THE COTTIN FLOODS OF JUNE 2007

*A Portrait in Words and Pictures
by Cottingham Residents*

Edited by Peter McClure and Tony Grundy

Cottingham Local History Society

**Dedicated to the flood victims of Cottingham,
their relatives and friends**

Published by the Cottingham Local History Society (2008)

ISBN 0-9544427-5-X

Printed by
Horsley and Dawson Ltd
72-73 Middle Street South, Driffield, East Riding of Yorkshire, YO25 6QF

CONTENTS

Page

Foreword *by Paul Hudson* v

Acknowledgements vi

List of photographic contributors vii

PART ONE: FLOODING IN COTTINGHAM

Pat Elliott   A brief look at past flooding 1

Peter McClure   The floods of 25 June 2007 and their aftermath 11

PART TWO: PERSONAL EXPERIENCES

1. JOURNEYS ON JUNE 25 23

Ann Hill   'It's raining, it's pouring….' 25
An adventure with the school meals run

James Hargreave   A clergyman's day in the flood 27

Mrs Rawling   A one-way journey by the scenic route [*] 29

Christine Gould-Knappett   When time stood still for a becalmed motorist 31

Peter McClure   Road closed 32

2. WEST COTTINGHAM 35

Ann Spence   Engulfed (*The Dales*) 37

Joan and Leo Murphy   Coming home to a near miss (*The Dales*) [*] 39

Justine Hunt   A devastating experience (*Eppleworth Road*) 44

Helen Bristow   Wine, wellies and a good book (*Rydal Grove*) 50

Richard Lambert   Saved by the moat (*West End Road*) 56

Liz Findley   Stress, mess and a change of address! (*West End Road*) 58

David Taylor   The Castle Hill surge (*Westfield Road*) [*] 65

Pat and Barry Johnson   Christmas in a caravan (*Southwood Road*) [‡] 67

3. CENTRAL COTTINGHAM   73

Sue Tidder   The day my mother cooked sausages! (*Crescent Street*) ‡   80

John Caley   My house in a river (*George Street*) *   84

Christine Moffat   My home in a skip (*George Street*) ‡   88

Alan Wright   George Place and the boat rescue (*George Street*)   92

Julian Savory   An unexpected day at home (*King Street*) *   96

Liam Potter   The ferocious flood (*Hallgate Junior School*)   98

Harold Mankel   A serious and very frightening experience (*Broad Lane Close*) 100

Gavin Smith   A cellar-full of Creyke Beck (*Station Road*)   106

Peter McClure and Val Barker   The Mill Beck flood (*Victoria's Way*)   110

4. NORTH COTTINGHAM   113

Dave Fairburn   Letter to America (*Linden Avenue*)   122

5. EAST COTTINGHAM   125

Bim and Sandra Pougher   We just lost everything (*Wanlass Drive*)   130

Fr John Leeman   The Snuff Mill Gates island (*Snuff Mill Lane*) *   141

6. SOUTH COTTINGHAM   143

Cyril Carter   The Snuff Mill tail-race (*Hornbeam Walk*) *   145

Pat Elliott   Some birthday! (*Hornbeam Drive*)   146

7. COTTINGHAM AFTER THE FLOOD   149

Pat Elliott   Out and about on June 26   150

APPENDIX

Peter Kerr   The Cottingham drainage system and some proposals for preventing future
                flooding   157

Map of the Cottingham area   167

* Indicates a story as told to Christine Gould-Knappett.   ‡ Indicates a story as told to Dorothy Catterick.

Foreword

Paul Hudson

Climate Correspondent and Broadcast Meteorologist, BBC Look North

The floods and extreme weather that affected much of Yorkshire in June 2007 were unprecedented. Throughout the month, the Environment Agency measured nearly 300 mm of rain in Hull, almost six times the monthly average of 50 mm. It turned out to be the wettest 12 day summer period on record and the resulting floods were devastating. Across the UK, the May to July period was the wettest since records began in 1766.

Put in perspective, the number of homes flooded across the East Riding of Yorkshire has been estimated at just over 6,000, compared with 5,000–6,000 across South Yorkshire and more than 8,600 within the city of Hull. Thousands of people were displaced, more than 3,000 in the East Riding alone. Hundreds of businesses and commercial properties were affected.

Cottingham was one of the many towns and villages in East Yorkshire that suffered serious flooding on June 25. This book by the Cottingham Local History Society is a memorable record of that extraordinary day and the traumatic consequences for people's homes and lives.

We can only hope that such extreme weather never happens again in our lifetime because, with a similar amount of rainfall in such a short space of time, the fear must be that, no matter what we do, flooding on a similar scale would be difficult to prevent.

24 June. *Storm clouds gather again over Cottingham. After a very wet summer, including heavy rain ten days earlier, more downpours start on the day before the floods. (John Horsley)*

Acknowledgements

The aim of this book is to record in words and pictures the devastating floods in Cottingham on 25 June 2007, and their aftermath. It is the result of a public appeal by the Cottingham Local History Society for photographs and personal stories, and the Society wishes to acknowledge its gratitude to everyone who responded.

The book was compiled and edited by Peter McClure and Tony Grundy, with the assistance of Dorothy Catterick, Pat Elliott and Christine Gould-Knappett.

This is not the first time that certain vulnerable parts of Cottingham have experienced flooding. There is a history to it, of which this book also offers a brief glimpse.

The photographs were edited by Tony Grundy, who was also responsible for the page layout of text and images. More than 1,250 colour images have been received from over 70 photographers, and have been stored in the Society's digital archive. From these about 470 photographs have been chosen.

The text was edited by Peter McClure. It includes 28 personal stories, which give a vivid picture of events, typical of those experienced by many Cottingham people on the day of the flooding and during the weeks and months that followed. The facts in the introductory chapters, the stories and the photo captions are as accurate as we could make them, bearing in mind that different people have their own experiences, perceptions and memories. More information may come to light after the book's publication and this may change our view of the facts in some of their details.

A knowledge of Cottingham's drainage system is essential to understanding what happened in June 2007. The editors are grateful to Peter Kerr, a chartered engineer (formerly with Yorkshire Water), for giving them his time, knowledge and advice so freely. He has been a key figure in the Cottingham Flood Action Group, exploring, photographing and mapping the drainage system and putting forward practical proposals for improving it.

Many people have had a hand in the making of this book. In addition to those named in the photographic credits and in the chapter and story credits, mention should be made of Dorothy Bell, Geoff Bell, David Brooks, Brenda Caley, Jim Davidson, Alex Duke, Yvonne Grundy, Teresa Hogan, Peggy Jaram, Fred Johnson, Katrin McClure, John McNicholas, Margaret Marson, Lesley Mather, Elaine Moll, Mr J Norris, Michelle Plater, Pat Raine, Doreen Raven, Alyson Shipley, Steve Walter, Ian Wright and Sylvia Wright. Thanks are also due to the staff of the East Riding Archive at Beverley and the Hull Local Studies Library.

The street plans used throughout the publication have been adapted from those of Clifford J Utting (2a Geneva Gardens, Romford, Essex) and are used with his permission.

Every effort has been made to trace the copyright holders of material produced in this book. If omissions have occurred the Cottingham Local History Society will be pleased to receive details for inclusion in any future edition.

A note on measures,   One inch = 25.4 millimetres (mm)

and approximately,   One foot ≈ 30.5 centimetres (cm)
One yard ≈ 0.91 metres (m)

One metre ≈ 1.09 yards ≈ 3 foot 3⅓ inches

List of Photographic Contributors

The following people have provided photographs of the flooding or its aftermath, and images of historical interest. Their names appear in brackets after the captions to the relevant photographs.

Denys Abba	Jean Durnford	John Hewgill	Chris Mead
Dave Acaster	John Dyet	Roger Hunt	Fiona Nicholson
Val Barker	Pat Elliott	Derek Jennings	Hilary Nowell
Peter Beal	Dave Fairburn	Barry Johnson	Julie Osgerby
Geoff Bell	Pete Featherstone	Glen Johnson	Mike Paddock
David Bird	Mike Fee	Terry Johnson	Steve Plater
Norman Bisby	Liz Findley	Peter Kerr	Dean Roberts
Mavis Bishop	John Frith	Julia Lambert	Walter Shelton
Andrew Brett	Shirley Fussey	Richard Lambert	Gavin Smith
Helen Bristow	John Garbera	Graham Latter	Sean Spencer
Hedley Brookes	Paul Gibson	Stuart Leadley	Martin Stroud
Geoff Burton	John Goodby	Martin Levitt	David Taylor
James Caley	Brian Goodison	Helen Leys	Chris Uney
Bryon Caley	Ken Green	Gwen Mathers	Stuart Walter
John Caley	Tony Grundy	Imogen Mathers	Ros Wareham
Dorothy Catterick	Tony Hailey	Geraldine Mathieson	Rachel Waters
Leslie Chicken	James Hargreave	Katrin McClure	David Woodward
David Clarke	Alan Hindley	Peter McClure	Chris Wright
Peter Conyers	John Horsley	Robert McMillan	

Note: Where times are available from digital camera photographs, these times have been assumed to be Greenwich Mean Time (GMT) and they have been corrected to British Summer Time (BST) when they are used in the captions for the pictures.

North Mill, Mill Beck

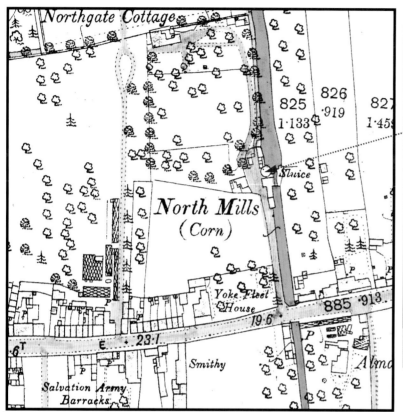

Map showing position of North Mill about 100 metres north of Northgate.
(Reproduced from O.S. 1892, 25" map)

THE OLD CORN MILL.
(From a photo belonging to Mr. Edward Archbutt Witty.)

A postcard view of North Mill in the 1880s. Originally a water mill, it was rebuilt as a hybrid wind- and watermill in the 19th century, and was pulled down in 1900. (Ken Green Collection)

__Autumn 1958.__ Culverting of Mill Beck from the site of the old North Mill down to Northgate began in the Autumn 1958 as part of the Mill Beck Lane housing development. The photo, looking north to the former mill site, shows the beck newly dug in preparation for the culvert pipe. At the bend of the road is a large 'FOR SALE' board. (CLHS Collection)

__Autumn 1958.__ A slightly later view of the same stretch of Mill Beck with the culvert pipe now in place. The trees and hedging have been chopped to reveal some of the buildings of the Lawson farm sited on Northgate. (CLHS Collection)

PART ONE

FLOODING IN COTTINGHAM

A Brief Look at Past Flooding

Pat Elliott

Introduction

Cottingham, seemingly, has always had a love-hate relationship with water. Its very location, on the eastern dip slope of the Wolds at the junction of the permeable chalk with the impermeable clay of the Hull valley and Holderness, gave rise to springs providing our forefathers with a valuable supply of fresh water. This water flowed through the settlement in open watercourses. Broadlane Beck and Creyke Beck fed the principal stream of Mill Beck, locally referred to as Cottingham Beck, which was harnessed to power water mills at North Mill, down Mill Beck Lane, and South Mill, later Snuff Mill. From there Cottingham Beck emptied into the River Hull at Stoneferry. To the east of the village the marshland of Cottingham Common offered summer pasture, fishing, wildfowling, reeds and turves for buildings. From medieval times until the late nineteenth century Cottingham extended to the River Hull, with access at Stoneferry affording transport and trading opportunities. Yet this proximity to the tidal River Hull, coupled with the lack of gradient for water flow and the heavy nature of the soil, could also be its downfall.

River Inundation

The low-lying nature of the land meant the ever present fear of flooding from both the River Hull and the Humber. In medieval times dykes, such as Setting Dyke, were constructed to take land water into the rivers, and banks were raised to keep out the tides. Nevertheless in 1265 the Humber floods reached as far inland as Cottingham. In 1352 there was widespread flooding and in 1356 the tides of both the Humber and River Hull were four feet above the norm. Winter inundations continued to be regular occurrences until the land was enclosed and systematically drained from the mid-to-late 1700s onwards. The parliamentary act of 1766 for Cottingham Common was both an enclosure and a drainage award. A new main drainage channel, Cottingham Drain, was cut to empty into the River Hull at High Flags, whilst individual fields, often with drainage ditches as boundaries, replaced the medieval system. Even so, high tides

The filling in of the Cottingham and Newland Beck at Cottingham Road and Fairfax Avenue in 1961. From Snuff Mill Lane to Fairfax Avenue the beck was replaced by the Cottingham Branch sewer, which fed into the Northern Branch trunk sewer at Fairfax Avenue. (Ken Green Collection)

could push water up the River Hull and into Cottingham Beck, causing flooding. The River Hull sluice could be shut, but this meant that water could not flow into it from Cottingham Beck, which would overflow. In 1961 the 20-foot wide beck was filled in from Fairfax Avenue onwards, and later in the same decade from Beck Bank to Fairfax Avenue. New large sewer pipes now took all of Cottingham's surface water straight to the Humber.

Springs and Becks

During wet winters and springs there has always been the risk of the becks overflowing, especially when tides were high. G H Hill, a schoolmaster living in Newland, wrote of Cottingham Beck in 1909: 'In recent years, before most of the houses were built, I have seen it a clear rushing torrent of clean Spring water, three feet deep'. The beck frequently spilled over its banks before it was partly filled in after the Second World War. Barry Cass recollects:

> 'Before the war I remember some fairly regular overflowing of Cottingham Beck near to where we live on Cottingham Road near to the Hull boundary. I had a school friend who lived in the terrace of houses with very long front gardens, between Fairfax and Kenilworth Avenues, and they were flooded quite frequently, rendering him very late or often unable to attend school. What an excuse, it beats the railway gates being shut!'

Part of an aerial view of Cottingham taken in April 1925, showing the hedge lines of Mill Beck and Broadlane Beck meeting behind the School grounds, just south (to the right) of a row of glasshouses. This open stretch of Broadlane Beck was later culverted when the School playing field was extended beyond the beck into the next field. (Aerofilms)

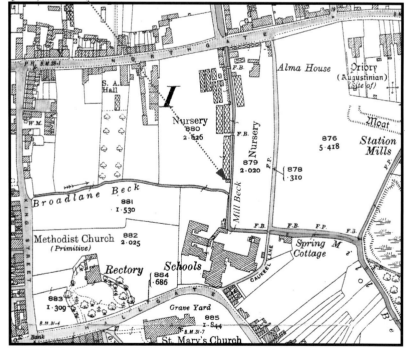

Mill Beck south of Northgate remained open until part of it was culverted for the Canongate housing development in the early 1960s. (Reproduced from O.S. 1910, 25"map).

Mill Beck at Beck Bank looking south towards Thwaite Street in the early 1900s. To the right are the grounds of Kingtree House. To the left is the garden wall of Cherry Garth, formerly Beck Bank House. (Ken Green Collection)

A postcard, probably from the 1920s, showing Mill Beck and Beck Bank from Newgate Street. (Shirley Fussey Collection)

Sewer pipes being craned into the bed of Mill Beck at Beck Bank (Summer 1966) The new sewer linked up with the 1961 Cottingham Branch sewer at Snuff Mill Lane. The wooden bridge across the beck gave access to the last house in this group of terraced houses, built in 1937. (Ken Green)

A postcard of Mill or Cottingham Beck as seen from Snuff Mill Lane, looking north. Top left is Bridge House, demolished in 1935. (Ken Green Collection)

Cottingham Beck looking south down Snuff Mill Lane in the early 1900s. To the right are the grounds of Eastgate House and beyond them a Dutch barn. (Shirley Fussey Collection)

An aerial view of Snuff Mill House, Snuff Mill Lane and Hornbeam Walk (an early 1970s development). The water mill was originally built for grinding corn but in the late 18th century it was used for making snuff. The mill was demolished in the 1930s but the house is still there. The mill leat and arch survived until 1961, when the beck from here to Fairfax Avenue was replaced by the Cottingham Branch sewer. (Ken Green Collection)

Creyke Beck was also liable to flood. In December 1960, residents of 'Creyke Lane' (now known as Dunswell Road) complained to the Haltemprice Urban District Council about flooding on the western side of the lane.

Whilst Mill (or Cottingham) Beck and Creyke Beck are fed by permanent springs, Broadlane Beck only flows after rainfall or when the intermittent springs along Eppleworth Road are active, the principal one being Keldgate Spring. *The Gentlemen's Magazine* of 1797 recorded Keldgate Spring as 'a noted spring about two yards in diameter, which breaking out in a ploughed land, utters an astonishing quantity of water, and will continue to do so for eight, ten, or twelve, or sometimes sixteen weeks, and then suddenly stop'. The author did not attribute rainfall as having any immediate influence as it could be two, three or seven years before erupting once more, generally in the springtime, when residents would recollect that 'Kell Gate Springs are broke out again'. A similar intermittent stream, the Gypsey Race, in the Great Wold Valley from Duggleby to Bridlington, prompted the superstition that these 'Waters of Woe' foretold some disaster. Thomas Thompson, in his residence of Cottingham Castle (now the hospital site), watched with interest the rise and fall of Keldgate Springs in 1821 and 1823, fearing it would flood his carrot fields, used to feed his livestock. He reasoned that 'there has been much snow this year, and its gradual thaw on the Wolds may have raised the Springs'.

The site of Keldgate Spring on Eppleworth Road. (Pat Elliott)

The Reverend Charles Overton noted in *The History of Cottingham* that the springs erupted again about Christmas 1852 after an autumn of 'unwonted inundation' and continued to flow for two or three months 'with astonishing rapidity'. They then lay dormant until 1860, 'a year much to be remembered for the amount of incessant rain that fell, from the beginning of spring, to the end of autumn'. This time they flowed for three or four months with the village pumps spouting water freely, whilst the handle remained still. A Professor Phillips at the time explained to Overton the similarity with springs in Wiltshire and Dorset. 'They are not drains of subterranean lakes, but overflows of a slowly arriving subterranean stream, received as rain drops, passing in capillary channels and collecting into a spring'. Overton recorded the Cottingham people's own explanation:

When Derwent flows
Then Keldgate goes.

G H Hill recollected meeting a Captain Henry Briggs about 1895, who told him that the springs had been measured at 6 million gallons a day, when in full flow. Yet Hill had also witnessed the springs dry or half-filled.

These springs have broken out intermittently in 1903, 1912, 1929, 1941, 1947 and 1960, according to A L W (Alex West?). Writing in the Cottingham Local History Society's Journal of March 1961, he noted that 1960 appeared to have been the wettest year on record, with recordings across the East Riding ranging from 28.96 inches at Cottingham waterworks to 36.68 at Hempholme lock (figures supplied by the Water Board and Hull River Board). On 5 January 1961 Keldgate Spring began to flow and other springs erupted 'for the first time for at least forty years'. Fields were waterlogged and crops lay unharvested. The River Hull had been at flood level for months, overflowing at each Spring tide.

There have been further instances of springs erupting in various parts of the village. Writing in 1909, Hill noted that when the new sewer and water mains were being laid 'in the curve of the road at

Cottingham', presumably near Bricknell Avenue junction with Hull Road, 'the springs in the gravel thereabout stopped the work for weeks'. He also recalled in the 1880s and 90s 'between this curve of the Road and Snuff Mill Lane, I have often seen the fields flooded across the road to the "Race" and the ice skated upon'. In spite of a lower water table nowadays, some springs are still active. Joan Cass reports:

> 'There are springs all around the Eppleworth Road/Castle Road area, one in particular being very visible and quite well known locally. This is situated at the first bus stop in Green Lane (southern end), where after heavy rain it bubbles up noticeably on the grassed area and runs in a shallow stream eastwards across the pavement and along the gutter into a drain. So if you're waiting for a bus there and it's been raining hard, prepare to skip about or don galoshes.'

The Dene, along Eppleworth Road, has an intermittent spring, which at times has filled it to the brim. In February 1955, for example, the Haltemprice U.D.C. noted that The Dene had flooded to a depth of seven feet, and councillors considered appointing an attendant to watch over children. The lake in Thwaite Gardens is partly fed by springs, which were bubbling up as recently as May 2008. No doubt local inhabitants can recollect other outbreaks.

March 2001. The Dene, fed by an intermittent spring, under water. (Pat Elliott)

August 2006. The Dene in its more usual dry state. (Pat Elliott)

Flash Floods

The most severe flooding in modern times has been the result of freak weather conditions. Although it did not make front page news, *The Hull Times* and the *Beverley Guardian* reported that on Wednesday 24 July 1912 there was a cloudburst, near Beverley, when an estimated two inches of rain fell in about two hours. Heavy rain, accompanied by thunder and lightning, started falling about two o'clock in the afternoon, before ceasing about four. Mr William Lawson, a milkman of Skidby, recounted that 'a tremendous cloud — as black as ink — came over the district and suddenly rain and hail fell as I have never seen it fall before. In a minute I was wet through.' Rabbits were drowned, fields flooded, turnips washed along the road and Eppleworth crossroads at the bottom of Castle Hill 'was a roaring torrent'. In Cottingham itself, 'the water rushed into the low-lying parts of the village, swamped scores of houses, flooded gardens and yards and rendered several streets impassable'. Houses near Coverdale Lane, i.e. Caukeel Lane footpath by Hallgate School, were marooned due to deep water and residents took refuge upstairs. Mill Beck, referred to as Cottingham Beck, was described as 'a mighty rushing torrent' sweeping everything before it — stools, tree branches, ashbins, rose trees and grass. In the hollow of King Street the water was four or five feet deep with Maria's Terrace flooded on the ground floor. As fast as the water was brushed out at the front it came in at the back. The water in George Street was also over four feet deep. 'A man had to take his horses and seven pigs, only 4 days old, out. Chickens were floating in the yards, and dogs frollicked in the flood.' A familiar photograph recording

24 July 1912. Postcards of children paddling at the junction of Crescent Street and George Street.
(Ken Green Collection, Rachel Waters Collection)

the event, shows children paddling, oblivious to the damage being caused. Furniture floated down the middle of South Street, whilst at the eastern end of Northgate towards Linden Avenue area a lake knee-

deep had built up, with cyclists and motorists amusing a crowd of onlookers, as they negotiated their way through. Mr Grotrian's residence, Westfield House (now The Fair Maid), had its grounds and gardens badly affected with, at one place, water seven feet deep. At the junction of Eppleworth Road and West End Road a stream seven or eight yards wide and two feet deep poured across the road. Mr J D Dunn, landlord of the Duke of Cumberland, was felled by the force of water as he endeavoured to cycle through. Yet by seven o' clock the flood had abated.

24 July 1912. Looking up George Street towards Northgate. (Norman Bisby Collection)

3 August 1984. Flooding in George Street seen from the junction with Crescent Street. (Walter Shelton)

George Street under water at the Crescent Street crossing, an undated photo, but certainly before 2007. It is thought to be no earlier than 2003. (Walter Shelton)

22 May 2006. Water flowing down into Canada Drive from the Willerby Low Road ditch. (Geoff Burton)

22 May 2006. Canada Drive, with flood water and fire engine. (Geoff Burton)

22 May 2006. The depth of the water in Dene Road, viewed from Eppleworth Road, is shown by the bow wave of the van. (Katrin McClure)

22 May 2006. Water pouring into the Dene from the pipe (left) that transfers excess water to and from the Eppleworth Road culvert. (Katrin McClure)

22 May 2006. Four fire engines and the police at the scene of the flooding at the east end of Eppleworth Road. (Katrin McClure)

The [Hull] Daily Mail recorded that torrential thunderstorms on Friday 3 August 1984 brought widespread flooding, with west Hull, Anlaby, Hessle and Cottingham the worst affected. The water was two or three feet deep in some places. Motorists abandoned their cars as roads became lakes, resulting in some roads being blocked. Manhole covers were lifted and holes appeared in a number of roads. In Cottingham four shops in King Street, plus the Duke of Cumberland pub, were flooded. The water in Jim Henderson's sports shop was four inches deep, with damage running into four figures. Photographs show that George Street was also flooded. As recently as 2006, flooding occurred again in Canada Drive and at the junction of Eppleworth Road and West End Road, after two days of heavy rain on May 21 and 22.

Such 'flash' flooding has not been restricted to the summer months. The front page of *The [Hull] Daily Mail* of 3 December 1937 proclaimed: 'Hull roads became rivers after the great rain' — 'Venice of the North' — 'Grave flooding dislocates traffic, maroons houses.' A gentle rain started falling about noon the previous day, gathering strength during the afternoon, and continued throughout the night

22 May 2006. A torrent of water in the ditch on the north side of Hallgate. (Katrin McClure)

and into the following morning. As this coincided with a high tide, the mains became choked and erupted onto the roads. The agricultural drains across Hull rose 'to an alarming level, and in many instances overflowed their banks'. In Cottingham the George Street area was closely monitored, having suffered serious flooding only a few years previous. When Cllr A Dixon, Chairman of the Haltemprice Urban District Council, visited houses in Southwood Road, he found some properties with water 18 inches deep and personally called out the fire engine and four men, who pumped out the water throughout the night. Incidentally, this was in the days before the fire service was nationalised and so 'free'. It would seem that Cllr Dixon may have called the fire brigade at his own expense.

Flash flooding sometimes precedes the eruption of Cottingham's springs. The 1947 eruption of Keldgate Spring was no doubt precipitated by melting snow, and both the snow melt and the spring may have contributed to flooding in the Eppleworth Road area in March 1947, as recorded in the Haltemprice Urban District Council minutes. The snow had lain several feet deep since January, during one of the coldest winters in recent times. Yorkshire (as with many other parts of England) experienced some of its worst floods ever at that time, with York and Selby under water from the River Ouse, which was seventeen feet above its normal height.

Conclusion

These few examples, of which there are many more, reveal that throughout time Cottingham has experienced flooding, whether this be from the springs, 'flash' flooding or tidal inundation. The village's very location means there is always a possibility that flooding will occur. With climate change experts predicting rising sea levels and more extreme weather conditions, the question everyone is asking now is 'How frequently will this happen in the future and what will be the scale of the resulting devastation?'

Sources

Anon.	*The Gentleman's Magazine* *Cottingham in 1797*, Malet Lambert Local History Reprints, 26
G H Hill	*The Township of Newland* (1909), Malet Lambert Local History Reprints, Extra Volume, 32
Anon.	*The Beverley Guardian*, 27 July 1912
Anon.	*The Hull Times*, 27 July 1912
Anon.	*The Daily Mail* (Hull), 3 December 1937
Anon.	*The Daily Mail* (Hull), 4 August 1984
Anon.	'The Keldgate Spring' *Cottingham Local History Society Journal*, 2, Pt 19, March 1961
K J Allison	*The East Riding of Yorkshire Landscape* (London, 1976)
K J Allison	*Cottingham Houses*, Cottingham Local History Society (2001)
Rev Charles Overton	
	The History of Cottingham (Hull, 1861)
A R B Robinson	*The Counting House, Thomas Thompson of Hull 1754–1828 & his Family* (York, 1992)
J Sheppard	*The Draining of the Hull Valley*, East Yorkshire Local History Society, 8 (1958)
I. McCaskill and P. Hudson	
	Frozen in Time: the Years When Britain Shivered (Great Northern Books: Ilkley, 2006)
D. Bielby	Unpublished notes from the Haltemprice Urban District Council minutes East Riding Archives (Beverley), U.D.H.A.1/2/20, 1/1/26 and 1/2/11

Personal recollections by Joan and Barry Cass
Information from Peter Kerr, Alex Duke and John D Markham

*Green Lane looking south from Eppleworth Road at
2.08 p.m. BST on 25 June. (John Frith)*

*West End Road looking towards the junction with Baynard
Avenue and Hallgate at 6.20 p.m. BST. (Dave Acaster)*

*Humber Rescue vehicles, fire engine and rescuers in George Street, looking
north at 8.45 p.m. BST. (Chris Wright)*

*Creyke Close under water on the
afternoon of 25 June. (Ros Wareham)*

The Events of 25 June 2007 and their Aftermath

Peter McClure

The floods of summer 2007 were shocking and in their severity they were unprecedented. As the previous chapter shows, Cottingham has suffered flooding many times in the past and mostly in the same places. Summer time flash floods can be as destructive as winter floods, the best known example occurring in July 1912, when cloudbursts flooded many places across England. The 1912 accounts of flooding in George Street, King Street, Caukeel Lane, Linden Avenue and the junction of Eppleworth Road and West End Road are strikingly similar to those in June 2007. If the devastation of Cottingham houses was more widespread in 2007 it is partly because there was more rain over a longer period, but also because houses have been built where few or none existed in 1912 — for example, in the Eppleworth Road/Castle Park area, West End Road, Creyke Close, Victoria's Way and Endyke Lane. Another difference is that all of Cottingham's surface water is now piped into the sewers. A bottleneck in the sewer system meant that water could not drain away.

The Events of Monday 25 June, 2007

There has never been a June quite like it. In fact it hardly stopped raining from May through to the last week in July. Flooding in Yorkshire in June was followed by flooding in Gloucestershire in July. The soaking we got in June broke all the records. A Met Office climatologist has told the Cottingham Local History Society:

> June 2007 was the wettest calendar month on record at several long running stations in Yorkshire, including Hull, Bradford and Sheffield. Hull recorded a total of 256.3 mm, which represents over four times the average amount for the month. The previous wettest calendar month at Hull was June 1982, which recorded 190.0 mm (rainfall records in Hull began in 1871). Cottingham also had its wettest calendar month with 244.7 mm, but records here only go back to 1983.

Two slow moving depressions produced exceptional rainfalls on June 13–15 and June 24–25. For June 14 (covering the time from 10 a.m. BST on the 14th to 10 a.m. BST on the 15th), the Met Office recorded 56.6 mm at the Cottingham weather station. This is around the month's average rainfall in a single day and it caused some flooding at the eastern end of Eppleworth Road. Further downpours over the next nine days meant that the ground was saturated when it rained heavily during Sunday the 24th, followed by an even more prolonged drenching on Monday the 25th, from the early hours of the morning until about nine in the evening. The Cottingham rainfall figures supplied by the Met Office are 25 mm for the 24th and 70 mm for the 25th. The Hull figures are 50.2 mm for the 24th and 63.0 mm for the 25th. Neither the ground nor the ditches and drains could absorb this monsoon of water falling from the sky. Three days earlier, anticipating the consequences, the Met Office issued an early warning of flood disruption in an arc from the Welsh Borders to 'Yorkshire and Humberside'.

The rain had nowhere to go except overground and downhill. Roads turned into rivers and low-lying properties into lakes. Cottingham was not alone. Hull, Anlaby and Hessle suffered extensive flooding, as did many East Riding villages. Flooding on the same day

June 24. King George V Playing Fields, when heavy showers falling on sodden ground were already forming lakes of water. (John Horsley)

elsewhere in Yorkshire (as in Sheffield and Doncaster) quickly got attention in the national media — and eventually Hull and the East Riding did, too.

Cottingham lies on sloping land between the Wolds and the River Hull flood plain, so although extreme weather events are far from common, when they do happen, Cottingham is vulnerable to flash floods. By mid-morning on June 25, so much water was pouring down the slopes of the Yorkshire Wolds that the A164 became impassable and had to be closed. The west-east roads from the A164 down into Cottingham (Castle Road/Southwood Road and Harland Way/Northgate) streamed with water. Everywhere in Cottingham, houses built in natural dips, at the bottom of slopes, or next to dykes, becks or ponds, were at risk of flooding, especially if the airbricks were at ground level or only a brick or two above.

Cottingham is also on the spring line. The pressure of flood water over an already saturated soil seems to have forced springs to break out from the aquifer. We have had reports of spring water appearing on June 25 in a garden in Westfield Road (David and Margaret Taylor), in Dene Road (Geraldine Mathieson), Eppleworth Road (Sylvia Wright), Station Mills (Gavin Smith) and under some houses in Linden Avenue (Trevor Brigham). It is likely that some well known springs were active, too, such as Keldgate Spring and The Dene spring, but we have no definite information about them.

Whether from rainwater or spring water, the drains, dykes and natural watercourses were overwhelmed. Water bubbled up from the road gullies to flood the streets and roads. The dyke on Willerby Low Road overflowed into the Canada Drive area, in spite of Council sandbags and pumping by the Fire Brigade. The dykes on Eppleworth Road and Linden Avenue flooded over into many of the adjacent properties.Broadlane Beck, Mill Beck and Creyke Beck broke their banks, inundating homes in Crescent Street, George Street, King Street, Broad Lane Close, Canongate, Creyke Close, Station Road, Victoria's Way, Dunswell Road, Wanlass Drive and North Moor Lane. Most of the problems were caused by water backing up from culverts and sewers that could not cope with the quantity of the water

Muddy water pouring down Eppleworth Road and across the junction with Green Lane. (John Dyet)

Creyke Close looking towards Canongate and St Mary's Church. (Martin Stroud)

trying to force its way through them. The open stretches of the becks and ditches can be more than six feet deep and considerably greater in width, while the culverts are at best 1.2 metres (4 ft) in diameter and are mostly narrower, down to 300 or even 225 mm (9 in). The pipes were therefore too narrow to receive all the water contained inside the banks of the open ditch or beck, and this was sometimes made worse by pipes being partially blocked with silt or rubbish. As one resident put it, 'It was like putting a quart into a pint pot'. Blocked road gullies may also have contributed initially to some local flooding. But the main problem was that the sewers had already become full by about eight in the morning, so none of the tributary drains and watercourses were able to flow into them. The lack of capacity in both the sewers and culverts explains why water was seen bubbling *out* of the gully sinks or forcing up the manhole covers over culvert inspection points.

A half-blocked 225 mm culvert under the east end of Eppleworth Road looking north, after the June floods. (Peter Kerr)

Half-silted-up culvert under Eppleworth Road near Castle Hill Hospital looking south, after the floods. (Peter Kerr)

A manhole cover in Crescent Street forced up by the pressure of the water in the surcharged culvert. (Stuart Walter)

To the east of the railway line, Kingdom Hall in New Village Road was flooded. Thwaite Lake expanded almost to the walls of Thwaite Hall and invaded Boardside Walk, spilling into New Village Road and Endyke Lane, where some properties were flooded on the north side. Further south, near Bricknell Avenue, Croxby Primary School was inundated to a depth of three feet and had to be abandoned. By late morning all the other village schools were closed, so that children could get safely home. The Humberside Police Station on Priory Road was flooded, as were the Clinic on King Street and the University's Lawns halls of residence on Harland Way/Northgate.

Some of the worst flooding occurred along the west-east, central spine of the village. It follows the line of a small valley, a mostly dry one in normal circumstances, but which created a powerful river of its own on June 25. The valley starts at Rowley, descending eastwards through Raywell and Eppleworth, until it broadens out along Eppleworth Road at the west end of Cottingham. The shallow valley here is interrupted by the defensive earthworks of Baynard Castle, beyond which it continues eastward between Hallgate on the south side and Northgate on the north until it peters out at the confluence of Creyke Beck and Mill Beck, an area west of Station Road long known as 'the Bogs'. Through the middle of the valley, from Crescent Street onwards, runs the bed of Broadlane Beck, an intermittent stream now mostly culverted, but the outline of the bed can be seen in the dip of the road in George Street and King Street and in the dip in the playing field behind the old Hallgate School buildings.

The King Street entrance to the Hallgate Schools, with the Clinic under water behind. (Mike Fee)

The west end of Eppleworth Road, looking west. Water unable to enter the culvert at the Keldgate Farm entrance (right) is spilling across the road. (John Dyet)

On June 25 the road from Raywell to Cottingham turned into a gigantic conduit for all the water pouring off the valley sides. At the A164 viaduct, more water cascaded over the bridge onto the road below. The nearby settling pond (designed to collect the runoff water from the A164) filled up and the excess water drained into the already overflowing ditch on the south side of Eppleworth Road. Further on, the culvert by the entrance to Keldgate Farm on the north side of Eppleworth Road could not cope, and water veered across the road into the houses opposite. To the west of these houses, rainwater was also pouring down from the Castle Hill Hospital building site into the purpose-built 'attenuation' ditch which collapsed and sent a wall of muddy water into properties on Eppleworth Road, The Dales, Green Lane and Sancton Close.

Eppleworth Road from the Sancton Close snicket looking west at about 7.15 p.m. BST. (John Frith)

The submerged back garden of Andrew Brett's house at the north end of The Dales, with the Hospital field beyond, where the attenuation ditch collapsed and sent a wall of muddy water into nearby properties. (Andrew Brett)

From Green Lane to West End Road, Eppleworth Road is a straight causeway, raised above the valley bottom to keep the road dry. Consequently the turbid brown water that streamed down the valley also ran off the road onto the land below on either side. On the north side some of it went into the dyke, which overtopped and flooded some properties lying next to it. But most of this river of water flowed off the south side of the road, where the valley is at its lowest, flooding most of the houses on that side of the road and also many houses in the adjacent roads (Stewart Garth, the north end of St Margaret's Avenue, Rydal Grove, The Ridings, Dene Road). The Dene pond overflowed, affecting some of the nearby properties.

Most houses on the south side of Eppleworth Road were flooded. (John Frith)

Through a rain splashed window on the afternoon of June 25. Water flooding into Stewart Garth. (Helen Leys)

St Margaret's Avenue looking south from Eppleworth Road at 7.24 p.m. BST. (John Frith)

West End Road looking north from the junction with Dene Road.. (Mike Fee)

At the bottom of Eppleworth Road and Dene Road deepening tides flowed across and down West End Road, which was eventually closed to traffic. Some of the water vanished into the old castle moat at the back of people's gardens and some of it travelled across the southern side of the castle earthworks, partly through the grounds of the old manor house and of Hillcrest House and partly into the ditch on Hallgate, where it powered into the culvert that goes under Crescent Street and George Street. Overground, a torrent of water in the grounds of Hillcrest House poured down into Crescent Street, where it was further amplified by underground water jetting out from the culvert manholes. Following the valley bottom along the former route of Broadlane Beck, this deluge sped with alarming force across George Street, through George Place (where the beck is open still) and onwards to King Street, where the beck is briefly open again by

This spectacular fountain was produced by water in the Crescent Street culvert forcing off the manhole cover. (Walter Shelton)

Water pouring like a waterfall through the gates of Hillcrest House into Crescent Street. (Stuart Walter)

Humber Rescue with an inflatable dinghy in George Street. (Chris Wright)

King's Court. There was severe flooding to many houses along this route and some residents had to be rescued by inflatable dinghy.

The 'river' continued across King Street and over the Hallgate School playing field. At the east end of the school grounds it joined forces with an open stretch of Mill Beck, at the point where the Broadlane Beck culvert (under the playing fields) was also discharging into Mill Beck. The result was widespread inundation of houses and/or gardens backing onto both sides of this part of Mill Beck

(Broad Lane Close, Canongate, Kirby Drive and Victoria's Way). Wooden boarding on the west side of Caukeel Lane bridge created a partial dam, which flooded one property in Broad Lane Close until a hole was made in the boarding in the early evening to let more of the water through. The problems were exacerbated by water from Creyke Beck, which joins Mill Beck north of Victoria's Way car park, not far from the gardens of the end houses in Kirby Drive. Nearby properties along Creyke Beck (in Station Road and Creyke Close) were badly flooded, as were the Station car park and the ground floor flats of St Mary's Mount in Station Road, east of Mill Beck. As Peter Kerr points out in the essay printed at the end of this book, all the surface water from the three becks passes through a coarse screen at the end of Victoria's Way, before it decants into the sewer at the junction of Hallgate, Victoria's Way and Beck Bank. During the morning of June 25, the entire sewer system became overloaded, so the water backed up, spilling over the banks of the open section of Mill Beck and of the southern end of Creyke Beck.

The flooding of Creyke Beck was so severe that many residents had to be evacuated. (Ros Wareham)

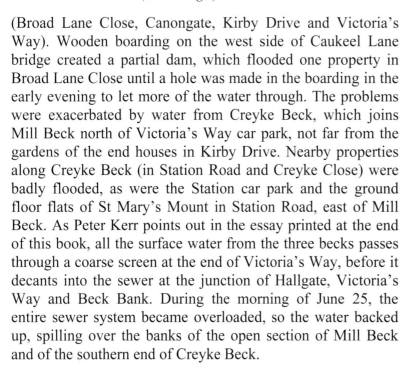

The submerged footbridge at the confluence of Mill Beck and Creyke Beck viewed from the snicket from Station Road along the back of the former Danish Bacon site (left). (John Horsley)

The east end of Hallgate near the junction with Beck Bank (right) and Station road (left, by the shop) . (Mike Fee)

Everyone who experienced the flooding talks of the frightening speed and volume of the water. Manhole covers were lifted off by fountains of water exploding from the culverts or drains below. Emergency phone lines were overwhelmed and the demand across the East Riding for sandbags and 'road closed' signs outstripped the ability to supply. Cars driving through flooding roads pushed waves of water into the ground floors of houses. A few drivers seemed to do it repeatedly, for fun. When neither the police nor the Council were able to close roads, residents did it themselves, making their own notices or parking vehicles across the road. Many householders fled upstairs with as many possessions as they could carry, before evacuating their homes altogether. Some people had to be saved by professional teams from the Humberside Fire and Rescue Service and Humber Rescue. The flooding happened so quickly and was so widespread that the emergency services were impossibly overstretched, and could only respond to extreme need and on an ad hoc basis.

A policeman accompanied by a paramedic directs a team from Humber Rescue towards flooded houses in George Street.
(Chris Wright)

The rain became intermittent in the early evening and stopped for good by about 9 p.m., but some roads still ran like rivers right through the night. Amazingly, next morning the becks and dykes were back within their banks and the road-rivers had vanished, except for a stream of water from Thwaite Lake across New Village Road. The world was quiet again.

The Aftermath

Appalling though the flooding was, the aftermath has for many people been an even more stressful experience. Close on 400 homes in Cottingham are known to have suffered significant ground floor damage from the flood water, and the toll on the physical and mental health of some householders, especially the elderly, has been a heavy one. Some flood victims evacuated to family or friends in

12 June 2008. A laden skip in Victoria's Way. The original electrical renovation was incompetent and dangerous so the ground floor rooms had to be stripped again. (Peter McClure)

Cottingham. Others less fortunate were taken to care homes in other towns, perhaps never to return. Homes have been wrecked and treasured possessions lost or ruined. Some people have been lucky with their insurers, loss adjusters and builders, others have not. There was inevitably a shortage of good, local builders. The sight of skips and caravans has been all too common in parts of Cottingham well into 2008. A year after the flooding, the nightmare is not yet over for some householders. There are houses still unoccupied or being renovated for a second time. After a wet Winter and Spring some homes that were dried out and refurbished have become damp again, with dank smells and mould growing on the walls. Some houses were renovated too early on poor advice, before being fully dried out, while others have been incompetently refurbished, with unsafe electrics or

__25 June 2008.__ A portaloo, a skip and a caravan at the west end of Eppleworth Road, a year later. (Peter McClure)

__25 June 2008.__ This caravan has served as kitchen and sitting room for the Featherstone family for a year, and will be for another month until the house is ready. Cold in winter, hot in summer, caravans are not easy places for long term daily living. Katie Featherstone says that what has frustrated her most is the slowness of the caravan cooker and not having her own washing machine. (Peter McClure)

botched plumbing, so they need stripping and renovating yet again. Flooded houses are proving difficult to sell. There are also householders who thought their homes had escaped damage only to discover nine months or a year later that the ground floor timbers are sodden and the plaster peeling off. The floods of 2007 have cast a long shadow.

In the face of such terrible events, the extraordinary indomitability of so many of the flood victims has been amazing. They in their turn talk about the immense kindness of neighbours and of the practical support given by voluntary organisations, such as the churches. With it have come new friendships and a much stronger community spirit. It is perhaps the one good outcome of an otherwise unmitigated disaster and thankfully the vast majority of houses in Cottingham (at least 95%) escaped damage even though their roads and gardens were under water.

Since June 2007 what has been uppermost in most people's minds has been the fear of a similar disaster in the future and the need to do something to prevent it. The Government set up a national review under Sir Michael Pitt, who published his report on the anniversary of the flood, 25 June 2008. The East Riding of Yorkshire Council set up its own Flood Review Panel, to take evidence from flood victims, from the Environment Agency and from Yorkshire Water, to examine the causes and consequences of the flooding right across the Riding, and to make recommendations to the Pitt Review. The report is dated May 2008 and it was adopted at a Full Council meeting on June 25. Hull City's two reports on the flooding by an Independent Review Panel (August and November 2007) are also relevant to Cottingham, since all Cottingham's surface water is currently disposed of through Hull's sewer system. Cottingham Parish Council has mounted its own review and made its own suggestions (published in April 2008). Cottingham residents have formed a Flood Action Group to put pressure on politicians and the agencies to sort out some better drainage management. One resident, Peter Kerr, a retired water engineer, has personally explored the ditches, becks, drains and culverts. He has come up with his own analyses and some possible solutions, published in a Cottingham Flood Action Group Newsletter, dated 9 June 2008. (See also Peter Kerr's essay in the appendix at the end of this book.) Two other relevant publications are a report on 'Flooding' by the House of Commons Select Committee on the Environment (May 2008) and a recent case study by the Environment Agency on the Hull floods.

The reports of the various bodies contain much information and analysis and many specific recommendations, too many to list here, and they need to be read in detail by everyone who has concerns about past and future flooding. It is fair to say that the quantity of rainfall between June 14 and 25 was far greater than any practicable drainage system could have handled and therefore some flooding was inevitable no matter what might have been done differently. Nevertheless, all the reports agree on two general criticisms.

The first criticism is that the drainage system could and should have functioned better than it did, thereby preventing the flooding of at least some homes and businesses. A key player is Yorkshire Water, for it supplies the sewer system through which the surface water from Cottingham, Willerby, Anlaby, Hessle and West Hull is conveyed via the Humbercare Tunnel out to Saltend. On June 25 parts of Cottingham were flooded because the sewer system was completely overwhelmed. The surface water and sewage that could not flow into the Cottingham Branch sewer backed upstream along the three becks, which broke their banks. Both the Hull and the East Riding reports criticise Yorkshire Water for inadequate funding, planning and operation of the sewerage system. In response the water company has set up a two-year dedicated flood recovery team and has promised a £16m investment, including an upgrading of pumping capacity at the West and East Hull pumping stations.

January 2008. Residents clearing Mill Beck at the Victoria's Way culvert, which takes water into the sewer under Hallgate and Beck Bank. (Val Barker)

It is generally agreed that there is a need for flood storage systems (lagoons, reservoirs, settlement ponds, attenuation ditches). Peter Kerr argues that an effective way of preventing another 'river' sweeping down Eppleworth Road through George Street and King Street would be for the Council to build an impounding reservoir on the west side of the A164 underpass. There is support in the Pitt Review, in the Parish Council report and in the Cottingham Flood Action Group newsletter for building such reservoirs to contain storm water, which can then be slowly drained away without swamping the drains, dykes, becks and sewers. The East Riding Council has responded by appointing consultants 'to undertake feasibility studies for provision of flood storage systems' (Report, p. 74). The NHS Trust has already built a larger and, we

The western end of the collapsed attenuation ditch on the Hospital building site south of Eppleworth road. (Andrew Brett)

hope, stronger attenuation ditch on the hospital site south of Eppleworth Road, replacing the one that was partly washed away on June 25. (An attenuation ditch slows down the rate at which surface water is released into the drainage system.)

An additional way of protecting the sewers from overload would be to channel some of the surface water in north Cottingham to the Barmston Drain. Following a request by the East Riding Council, 'the possible diversion of land drainage from the sewer system is being considered as part of the Environment Agency river Hull strategy' (East Riding Flood Review Panel Report, p. 74).

All the reports also acknowledge that the local drainage system of road gullies, ditches, becks, culverts and screens needs better monitoring and more frequent and thorough cleaning. The agencies have been visibly doing their bit during 2008. The Environment Agency has de-silted stretches of Mill Beck and Creyke Beck. The East Riding Council has cleaned all the gullies and employed a specialist firm to clear Cottingham's culverts. Unbelievable quantities of silt and rubbish have been extracted

The early-nineteenth-century brick culvert under George Street. (Peter Kerr)

5 June 2008. The culvert in Crescent Street being cleaned. Notice the pile of old bricks by the tree. (Peter Kerr)

(June 2008). One wonders when the old brick culvert in Crescent Street (built *c.*1804) was last properly cleared. A ton of old bricks and 26 tons of silt were removed from it, as well as ancient litter such as a World War Two fizzy drink bottle, according to one account. Residents report that the culvert and sewer appear to be damaged and the contents mixing, requiring a new culvert and sewer. Some of the culverts in Cottingham also need replacing with larger pipes, though this is complicated by the fact that some are privately owned, taking water under house driveways and frontages.

The second main criticism is that the current management of the drainage system is disjointed and incoherent. It is split between several parties with different agendas, uncoordinated responsibilities and little history of cooperation. In the East Riding there are five principal parties. **Yorkshire Water** is responsible for the public sewers and has a statutory duty to receive storm water from water customers. **The Environment Agency** has permissive powers to manage flood risk from main rivers. Permissive powers are those which are exercised only with the permission of the landowner. The EA has the power to dredge the open stretches of Mill Beck and Creyke Beck but not to look after their banks or dispose of any rubbish. Historically it has not had any responsibility for Broadlane Beck, though this may now change. **The East Riding of Yorkshire Council** is responsible for road drainage and also has permissive land drainage responsibilities for ordinary watercourses. It provides the screens or grills for the culverts on Cottingham's becks and dykes. **The Internal Drainage Boards** have permissive land drainage responsibilities for ordinary watercourses and open drains on private land, but the Haltemprice area no longer has one, so the East Riding Council takes on that responsibility in Cottingham. Finally there are the **Riparian Owners**.

Riparian owners are owners of land on the boundary of a watercourse. In the residential areas of Cottingham most of them are ordinary householders, few of whom were aware that they had a legal obligation to accept flood flows and look after the beds and banks of part of any beck or ditch that runs either inside or alongside the legal boundaries of their own property. The obligation can be unjust to individual house owners and seems a hopelessly inefficient way of keeping these watercourses maintained (*cf.* the MPs' Select Committee Report, Summary §26). To add to the confusion, it is a matter of dispute whether some watercourses, open or culverted, are under riparian ownership or the Council's. Some residents think that this responsibility would be better met if it were removed to one agency, such as the East Riding Council, and the cost of looking after these ditches shared by us all through Council Tax or the Parish Precept. However, the East Riding Flood Review Panel assumes that

A culvert in the ditch at The Woodlands on Harland Way (looking west), after the June floods. The ditch is partly silted up, overgrown and a dumping place for schoolchildren's lunch discards. (Peter Kerr)

The diameters of culverts, like this 300 mm one under a driveway on the north side of Eppleworth Road, are usually small in comparison with the dimensions of the open ditch. (Peter McClure)

riparian responsibilities will continue as before, recommending that 'details of riparian ownership should be included in Home Information Packs and that legislation should be introduced to require this by law' (Report, p. 3, §2.13). It also recommends that 'the Council and the Internal Drainage Boards should identify riparian ownership of critical watercourses and work to ensure that these are adequately maintained' (Report, p. 5, §2.40). This appears to be an admission that no-one knows who is

responsible for looking after certain stretches of watercourses. The Council has appointed an additional drainage engineer 'to work with, educate and where necessary take enforcement action against riparian owners' (Report, p. 27, §14.7.9).

This is a very simplified account of the complexities and uncertainties of the current arrangements, and does scant justice to the detailed analysis and many recommendations of the reports. One of the East Riding's main recommendations is that the Environment Agency should be given more statutory duties, more powers and more resources to protect us from flooding. The Pitt Review goes further, proposing that the Environment Agency should be 'a national overview for all flood risk, including surface and groundwater flood risk' (Pitt Review, Executive Summary, p. xii, Recommendation 2), a proposal welcomed by the EA. However, this would not resolve the problem of divided responsibilities, which the Pitt Review and the MPs' Select Committee urge the Government to sort out. It is perfectly illustrated by Mill Beck at Victoria's Way, from where it decants into the sewerage system. Four different parties (the Environment Agency, the riparian owners, the East Riding Council and Yorkshire Water)) are involved in an uncoordinated management of a few yards of water. The East Riding report has responded by recommending the establishment of 'a multi-agency Flood Protection and Resilience Board' for the area (Report, p. 3, §2.1). Its function would be to oversee the whole system in a coherent way and ensure effective, coordinated action from the different agencies. We can only hope, with the Pitt Review (p. xx, Recommendation 28), that a single unifying Act of Parliament will be passed as soon as possible to rationalise and clarify drainage responsibilities and to increase the powers of the agencies to protect us from flooding. In the mean time the Cottingham Parish Council and the Cottingham Flood Action Group will no doubt keep up the pressure for measures that will actually work in Cottingham.

The probable recurrence of a summer storm event like that of June 25 is estimated to be something like once in every 150 years based on Yorkshire Water figures or over 200 years based on Met Office figures. As Hull's Interim Report points out (pp. 8–9), statistical probabilities are not predictions of actual frequency and these figures are in any case based on slender historical data. With luck it may be several generations before a similar threat of flooding comes out of the blue to terrify Cottingham people and devastate the lives of flood victims. But we cannot rely on wishful thinking, especially when climate experts believe that extreme weather events are likely to become more frequent as the century progresses. Some adults and children are still traumatised by what happened last June. For them and for many others who suffered from flooding, rain stirs instant alarm, especially if it is prolonged or intense. This fear will only be significantly reduced when people can see that the drainage system and its management have been radically improved.

Sources and References

This account of the floods is largely based on information from local residents. Comments on the drainage system are indebted to information and advice from Peter Kerr, but the interpretation is the responsibility of the author. The chapter also makes use of the following sources:

Met Office   *Summer 2007 Floods — case study*
www.metoffice.gov.uk/corporate/verification/case_studies.html

Met Office   'Weather news'
www.metoffice.gov.uk/climate/uk/interesting/

Met Office   Weather station records for Yorkshire, including Sheffield, Bradford, Hull and Cottingham (personal communication)

Michael Fish, Ian McCaskill and Paul Hudson, *Storm Force* (Great Northern Books: Ilkley, 2007)

Yorkshire Water Press statement, 20 November 2007

HM Government, 'Planning Policy Statement 25: Development and Flood Risk', p. 36, Table 2.1, 'The range of responsibilities and accountabilities of those involved in managing surface water drainage'
www.communities.gov.uk/planningpolicystatements/pps25

The Pitt Review: Lessons learned from the 2007 floods
www.cabinetoffice.gov.uk/the pittreview.aspx

House of Commons Environment, Food & Rural Affairs Committee, 'Flooding', 5th Report of Session 2007—08, vol. 1 (London: The Stationery Office Limited, 7 May 2008)

Environment Agency, '2007 Summer floods: tackling surface water flooding in Hull'
www.environment-agency.gov.uk/2007summerfloods/

Hull Independent Review Body, *The June 2007 floods in Hull, Interim Report* (24 August 2007)
Final Report (21 November 2007)
www.coulthard.org.uk/downloads/floodsinhull3.pdf

East Riding of Yorkshire Council, *Report of the Flood Review Panel* (June 2008)

Cllr Katrin McClure. 'Flooding in Cottingham 2007: an account of the events with questions to be considered by the Flood Review Panel' (a submission to the East Riding of Yorkshire Flood Review Panel)

Cottingham Parish Council, 'Response from the Cottingham Parish Council to the flooding in June 2007'. *Cottingham Times*, 77 (April 2008), p. 9

Cottingham Flood Action Group Newsletter, 9th June 2008

PART TWO

PERSONAL EXPERIENCES

1. Journeys on June 25

Journeys in and out of Cottingham became increasingly difficult on June 25. Some western routes in and out of Cottingham were blocked to traffic when the A164 between the Castle Hill and Willerby roundabouts was closed by police because of flooding. The A63 was also closed. For getting to and from Hull, Priory Road became hazardous, while Newland Avenue and Chanterlands Avenue were impassable. Only Cottingham Road provided a safe but congested route.

Hull, 25 June. *Chanterlands Avenue looking south towards the railway bridge. (David Bird)*

Hull, 26 June. *Priory Road looking south from Arden Close at 1.55 p.m. BST. Priory Road was closed for several days. (John Frith)*

The A63 near Brough on 25 June. The road was eventually closed. (Simon Mills, 'Storm Force' - Great Northern Books)

'It's Raining, it's Pouring . . . .' An Adventure with the School Meals Run

Ann Hill

Executive Head Teacher at Hallgate Infant School, Cottingham

Monday 25 June

11.30. It has rained heavily since I set off for work early this morning. Steve, the delivery man from Willerby, set off as normal from our school with the hot school meals which are cooked in our kitchen, put into Thermoports® to keep warm, and delivered to Willerby Carr Lane Junior and Infant schools.

11.50. Steve returned with the school meals. He was shocked by the rapidly forming floods and disappointed that he was unable to drive through them to make his daily delivery.

11.55. I asked my admin staff to contact all parents and inform them that with rapidly rising water levels it would be prudent to collect their children after lunch.

12.10. A member of staff volunteered to drive her 'off road' vehicle to deliver the meals to the Willerby schools. I thought this was a brilliant idea! We ran backwards and forwards, through the torrential rain, quickly loading the Thermoports®. We set off with Barbara Caws, the school cook, who was anxious that the hot meals should arrive safely. Some had to be nursed on our knees as there was little room inside the vehicle! I assured staff that we would return within the hour....

12.55. Alarm bells began to ring, as a journey that normally takes five minutes had already taken three quarters of an hour. We were queuing, travelling uphill against the flow of a small river which had formed on Castle Hill Road opposite the hospital. The traffic was moving at a snail's pace. Everyone was calm, waiting patiently and mesmerised by the deepening water from the heavy rainfall.

13.00. At last we arrived at the roundabout on the A164 to be greeted by a police officer who directed us to turn right towards Beverley! We lowered the driver's window and explained our plight, saying we were on a mission to feed hungry school children. The officer was compassionate. She allowed us to turn towards Willerby, which was directly into a rather deep flood! Our colleague straightened her body, as if preparing for a battle,

Southwood Road at about 2 p.m. on 25 June, with a long tail of traffic stretching up Castle Road to the A164. By this time the police had closed the A164 between Castle Hill and Willerby. (Hedley Brookes)

took a deep breath and changed gear into 'water' mode, I believe. Barbara and I grasped our seats and held our breath! We were elated when our colleague drove confidently, over the kerb, off the road, avoiding the very deep part of the flooded area.

14.00. Queuing was to become a major part of the **seven hour journey.** Throughout that time we witnessed many acts of kindness and camaraderie. We saw many vehicles being abandoned in deep water, their drivers obviously resigned to the inevitable. The most disappointing part for us was that we were unable reach our destination, blocked by the deepest of floods in Willerby old village. Some local people warned us that around the corner they were sailing a dinghy! It was at this point that we decided to return to Cottingham with the rapidly cooling school meals. So, reluctantly, we drove up to higher ground, turned around, driving back through fast flowing brown rapids, unable to see the road, continually fearful of any hidden dangers.

15.50. After attempting several different routes back to school, only to discover that the roads had been closed, we began to despair a little. However, as we tried to cut through from Willerby onto Priory Road, a journey of two and a half hours, the queue ground to a halt. I was wearing wellingtons and a waterproof coat, so I ventured from the comfort of our vehicle to investigate the problem. Half a mile

Willerby, 25 June. Routes into and out of Willerby were blocked by floods. This picture shows Kingston Road under water. (Derek Jennings)

Hull, 25 June. The entrance to Springhead Park Golf Course on Willerby Road, just within the Hull boundary. (Derek Jennings)

down the queue I met a police officer, who was directing traffic to turn around and 'find a little café for shelter and food'. As we had lots of delicious food, albeit a little cool, in our vehicle we decided to nourish ourselves on the jacket potatoes and chocolate sponge pudding! The reality that we may not be returning to Cottingham for some time had hit us . . . by now the school was closed. Trying not to sound too much like the intrepid explorer Scott, we used our lifeline, our colleague's mobile phone, to suggest to colleagues that they went home as there was nothing more they could do — we may not return for some time. Staff left the school after alerting our families as to what was happening.

19.15. I began to feel a little desperate whilst our colleague optimistically drove us up and down narrow lanes all around the countryside of Swanland, Raywell and Willerby. After each journey we returned to the same place — Great Gutter Lane! During this period our colleague had several conversations with her husband on her mobile phone. We took his advice, which meant ignoring a 'closed road' sign in an attempt to return to Cottingham through the flooded route from Raywell to Eppleworth Road. He

advised us that because of the deep dykes on either side of the road, it may be passable with care. It was (!), although it was frightening to see several abandoned vehicles floating alongside the hedges. We felt lucky and were thrilled to be finally returning to Cottingham after **seven hours!** My car was the only vehicle in the flooded car park behind Cottingham Clinic. I dashed into school, grabbed my keys and quickly moved it to higher ground. The rain continued to be torrential. I had had enough excitement for one day and was pleased when Barbara offered me a bed for the night at her house, as I was unable to drive home.

What happened to the school meals? No, we didn't have them for supper!

Hallgate Junior School playing field submerged by the overflowing of Broadlane Beck and Mill Beck. Wasdale Green bungalows are in the background. (Mike Fee)

A Clergyman's Day in the Flood

James Hargreave

As a locum chaplain at Castle Hill Hospital I spend Monday mornings with my colleagues planning the week ahead. When the weather is fine I usually cycle, both to burn off a few calories up Castle Road and to relieve pressure on parking spaces. The morning of 25th June seemed to me a little overcast, and in view of the fact that I was due to conduct the funeral of a friend's mother at Haltemprice Crematorium, I needed to make the journey by car in order to transport my clerical robes.

As the funeral was due to start at 12 noon, I set out from Castle Hill Hospital car park at 11.15 a.m. just in case of the unforeseen. (Little was I to know what lay ahead, literally round the corner!) Although it was raining, I experienced no undue concern. However, at 11.45 a.m. I became extremely anxious to find myself stuck behind an enormous queue of traffic on Castle Hill. In contravention of the Highway Code I used my mobile phone to warn the Crematorium staff of the strong possibility of my late arrival for the service, only to be told that the funeral procession coming from Driffield was also experiencing severe delay. My relief was short-lived. When I turned the corner into Beverley Road, the full extent of the problem became obvious. Looking down the short stretch of road to the entrance of the Crematorium, I had to contemplate the possibility of my engine being swamped by the waters of what was rapidly becoming the Beverley 'lake'. I took the risk, and driving past several abandoned cars, arrived at the Crematorium with vehicle unscathed.

Duly robed for the service, I began an hour's wait for the arrival of the cortège, watching the deluge with a sense of awe and concern for my friend and his family. Having learnt that all subsequent funerals on that day were to be cancelled, I was greatly relieved to have been able to conduct the service for my friend's mother without incident. However, the arrangements for the funeral tea, due to be held at Willerby Manor, were to be complicated by the fact that the road was impassable. After some frantic phone calls my friend, who had contacts in the entertainment industry, arranged for the venue to be switched to the Ramada Jarvis. The management kindly opened the entrance on the Willerby Low Road, enabling all the guests, including myself, to gain access. On arrival in the hotel, we soon realised the seriousness of the situation when we saw the news bulletin concerning the poor young Hessle man trapped in a gulley. After the meal, where I met many old friends, I decided to make for home, knowing that the Beverley Road route would not be possible. Following a small convoy of vehicles down the Willerby Low Road, I thought I was home and dry(!) until I reached the junction with Castle Road, where my way was blocked by a tape and a fire engine positioned in front of the newly formed lake. After negotiation with the fire officer a lucky few of us were guided through the waters, enabling my safe return to base. I was to learn that my friend and his family who live in Lincolnshire had an enforced night's stay in the hotel, and that the undertaker arrived home at 7.30 p.m.

25 June, 1.31.p.m. BST. Junction of Willerby Low Road and Castle Road partially blocked by fire engine pumping flood water out of the dyke into a manhole. (John Frith)

Not being a person to be deterred by a rain shower, I decided to make the journey to Hull University, where I attempt to inspire schoolchildren with a love of Latin. I did not want to let down one particularly dedicated pupil who had a 100% attendance record, enduring all weathers to learn his *amo, amas, amat*. I braved the journey along a flood-free Cottingham Road only to find the corridors of academe deserted. I am glad that my pupil made up for the dint in his attendance record at a later date. That evening the flood relieved me of chairing the AGM of the Hull Bach Choir, and instead I joined

Looking west from George Street towards the 'fountain' in Crescent Street (west). Alex Duke's car parked across the road to block traffic in George Street. (James Hargreave)

Fire Brigade and Humber Rescue in George Street with dinghy. (Chris Wright)

the crowd at the corner of George and Crescent Streets to watch the mounting level of the waters. By 8 p.m. the manhole covers in Crescent Street West had been lifted off by the water pressure, giving rise to a fountain at least ten feet high. A fire engine was soon on the scene, as well as Land Rovers bringing dinghies to facilitate the evacuation of elderly residents living in the flats. I was amazed to see vehicles attempting to drive through the lake which had formed in the dip in George Street, and angry that the wash they created compounded the flooding in the houses already affected. Fortunately the driver of a 4x4 used his vehicle as a barrier to prevent a recurrence of this problem. By this time a torrent of water was flowing down Crescent Street outside my house, at a level of one inch below the kerb; I gingerly used a bin bag to block the air bricks of my end terrace house, knowing that realistically nothing could hold back the force of nature.

Looking north down George Street from the corner of Crescent Street. (James Hargreave)

Water rising over the pavement in Crescent Street (east). (Chris Wright)

Within a shorter time scale than that of Noah, I was able to breathe a sigh of relief when the waters subsided, at the same time feeling great sympathy for my near neighbours affected badly, presumably on account of the lower level of their homes. However, I was not to escape damage completely. A few days after the event, looking up at the ceiling of my spare room, I noticed a strange pattern, which was not part of the original decoration: the rain had forced its way under a loose tile and caused the offending stain. Until the redecoration that stain will continue to be a tangible reminder of that June day in 2007, which I am sure will remain for ever in the memory of the people of Cottingham.

A One-way Journey by the Scenic Route

Mrs Rawling

I live in East Cottingham and, although there was a little flooding around, I escaped except for a sunken rockery in my garden, which briefly was transformed into an attractive pond. But my experience on the Monday involved spontaneous travel!

I had arranged to pick up my grandchildren from school that day, and during the morning it was raining heavily and I attended a funeral amid all the downpour. On the car radio I heard about incipient flooding, and shortly afterwards that schools were closing, including the one from which I had to collect my charges. I went home and changed quickly, and set off at about 11.30 a.m. Although the roads were running with water, I got as far as Castle Road roundabout to go to Willerby, aiming for the Swanland area. I discovered that there was no left turn, as the road was closed, and long traffic queues had built up. Thereafter, it was a catalogue of trial and error . . . .

I turned right for Skidby to approach Swanland from another direction. Skidby was badly flooded but I managed to drive through the deepish water. I thought I might have tried Eppleworth Road, but traffic was not allowed down there. I headed for Little Weighton, where there was some water maybe a couple of feet deep, but I got through and turned left for Rowley.

Willerby, 25 June. Riplingham Road from the junction with Great Gutter Lane.
(Sean Spencer/Hull News & Pictures Ltd)

It continuously pelted with rain and there were rivers flowing all over the roads. I arrived at the school at about 1.30 p.m. and collected the children, and took them home. I then stayed with friends in Swanland village, where the pond had extended all over the road, until about 7.15, thinking that the rain and flooding would have cleared and there would be less traffic.

Swanland, 15 June. The pond overflowed, nearly reaching Christ Church, and formed a river running down Main Street past the parish church of St. Barnabas. Conditions on June 25th were similar. (Graham Latter)

I left to journey back to Cottingham, hoping to re-trace my route, but various roads were closed, so I returned towards Swanland to try Tranby Lane. But Anlaby was also flooded, so I went to Kirkella, where again I found water on the roads, but got through safely. Turning left for Willerby, I came upon heavy traffic moving slowly. Just past Gorton Road everything slowed to halt, remaining stationary, and I was trapped in a long line of traffic. I saw a very wet cyclist riding past the line of vehicles. Apparently he couldn't get through because after an interval he came back, talking to drivers as he went past (like the dove from Noah's Ark!). Some vehicles in front, near to an intersection, turned round and came back the other way. As space became available, all the traffic followed.

Anlaby, 25 June. Rokeby Park, between Boothferry Road and Anlaby Road, was impassable. This car had to be abandoned. (Chris Mead)

North Ferriby, 25 June. Brickyard cottages in Church Road. (Graham Latter)

Hessle, 25 June.
(Sean Spencer/Hull News & Pictures Ltd)

I wondered whether to try to back-track to Hull and approach Cottingham that way, but it was now after 8.30 and it had never ceased pouring with rain. Roads were running with surface water or flooded. I still did not know of a safe route into Cottingham even from just a few miles away. No-one seemed to know what was happening in the local area (not even the controllers re-directing traffic) and certainly there was no sound information on the wider picture. Even with mobile phone communications and radio updates, the situation was changing all the time. I have heard since that the Hessle direction was also affected, with the Clive Sullivan Way awash on both carriageways nearer Hull and impassable.

So I made a few arrangements by phone, and went back to Swanland, never reaching home! I left quite early the next morning and had no trouble travelling on any of the roads. I had radio, a phone, helpful contacts and fuel, and in my case there were not serious problems, but I am sure that some people must have been very greatly inconvenienced. Indeed an acquaintance had to abandon her car and walk or wade to safety, and deal with its collection the next day.

When Time Stood Still for a Becalmed Motorist

Christine Gould-Knappett

The avenues where I live, near Hymers College in West Hull, did not suffer any flooding but there was continuous heavy rain, causing large puddles and waterlogged verges. Parts of the College playing fields were just a vast expanse of water. I had planned to approach Cottingham via Priory Road, but Perth Street West was impassable, and we were directed along Park Avenue in a slow one-way crocodile, funnelled in from various directions because of flooding, mainly under Chanterlands Avenue railway bridge.

A little way along, water was pooling and then, suddenly, axle deep and more. Everything stopped, and we were stranded in a stationary line in a foot or so of water. Some vehicles had stalled or taken in water and, abandoned, were causing obstructions on the road. Some had been able to pull

Hull, 25 June. *Chanterlands Avenue looking north towards the railway bridge.*
(Mike Paddock)

on to the verges — or where the drivers thought the verges were. It was a lake, awash with water across the road and into the front gardens. There seemed to be no pedestrians, but when one car attempted to manoeuvre, a resident appeared, anxious that the wash would enter his property. We were stuck thus for what seemed an age, but was probably not all that many surreal minutes.

I was obviously going to be late, but my phone was in a handbag on the rear seat, and out of reach. I didn't wish to open the door because, although my vehicle is fairly high, the water seemed to be about sill-level. Also I felt it prudent to keep the engine running at a brisk idle, and the summer-shod feet occupied and safe inside, unless there were some urgent development.

It was strange to be helplessly marooned, the most disconcerting aspect being lack of communication — we were locked immobile and silent in a row, each an isolated dry pod, and no-one knew what was happening. There was general information on the local radio, but even the people who re-directed us were not aware of the changing situations in other areas. We didn't know how long we would be there, or whether indeed we could continue.

Shortly there was some slow forward movement and we gradually cleared the flood; then a long wait to gain the already nose-to-tail crawling traffic on Princes Avenue — just erratically popping out at someone's goodwill. Other routes ahead were also frustrated by areas having become impassable — Newland Avenue in my case — and this long, dripping procession of assorted vehicles wound its way at a snail's pace along Queen's Road to join traffic, a car or two at a time, on a congested Beverley Road. After this the driving conditions, although slow, were much improved, and I was able to turn into Cottingham Road to eventually reach my destination. I suppose that the journey to Cottingham must have taken an hour or so, and I returned home by a similar route avoiding the known barriers without too much delay.

My experience was on a very small scale when compared to some of the road conditions encountered by others, and yet the cameo left a major impression on me. I was on familiar territory and only yards from 'dry' ground — the flooded section later proved to be quite short. But I did not know the timing or route to be taken for my destination — an unusual little vacuum of unreality. We are used to unthinkingly taking order and stability for granted, and it felt a bit unpredictable, like the atmosphere must have been during the War! Fortunately it was only an inconvenience to me, but I'm sure that some people must have been seriously delayed.

Road Closed

Peter McClure

June 15. Rokeby Park in west Hull where, as in Cottingham, some roads experienced flooding. (Chris Mead)

On Monday June 25, 2007, my wife Katrin and I were coming home from a ten-day holiday in Switzerland. It had been mostly sunny and dry there — thank heavens, we thought, because on our last trip there in August 2002 we'd had ten days of almost unbroken rain. Great for the waterfalls, but not for the walking, bird-watching, flower and butterfly hunting. The weather was so bad then that, on the day we left Switzerland in 2002, the rivers were almost over the bridges; it was, in fact, the start of major flooding across Europe. So five years later we were flying back to Manchester from Zurich on June 25 feeling lucky that atrocious weather hadn't dogged us a second time. We were totally unaware of what had been happening at home, that on June 15, the day we flew from the airport, parts of Cottingham had been flooded, especially in Eppleworth Road, near our house in West End Road, and that even worse flooding was happening while we were travelling home again.

We flew into Manchester airport at about six in the evening and saw the familiar grey skies but no rain. We asked the bus driver what the weather had been like in England. 'Oh, it's rained a bit', he said, 'and there's been a bit of flooding in a few places'. We collected the car, had a meal and started to drive home at about eight o'clock, reckoning to arrive in Cottingham by 10.30 at the latest. We didn't get home until midnight.

It was while we were on the motorway, passing Goole, that we saw the overhead warning sign: M62 CLOSED AT JUNCTION 38. That's the North Cave exit, we thought — there must have been a crash — we'll have to go off there. We turned on Radio Humberside but the bulletins told us very little, except for the surprising news that the M62/A63 had been closed because of flooding. When we got to Junction 38 we could see a queue of stationary cars ahead on the M62/A63, and another one snaking up the slip road to North Cave. We joined the North Cave queue, but when we got to the top of the slip road, we met a temporary ROAD CLOSED sign barring the way to North Cave. The traffic was being directed to the right, across the bridge, by a man in a glow-jacket, who told us to follow the car in front, which was going to Willerby. We never saw that car again.

Aiming for South Cave, we drove down into the night towards Broomfleet, along narrow country lanes. At least it wasn't raining, but it was pitch black and we no longer quite knew where we were. We splashed through small lakes and across impromptu streams, past the dark shape of a farmhouse surrounded by water, with a pump spewing water into the road. An abandoned car suddenly loomed into the headlights by the hedge side. It was a great relief when at last a junction road sign pointed us to South Cave. A bridge took us back across the A63, into the aptly-named Water Lane, but at the end of it, Church Street in South Cave was blocked by another ROAD CLOSED sign . So we had to turn round, cross the A63 again, turn left and join the A1034, which took us back over the A63 into South Cave's main Street (Brough Road). From there, to our intense relief, we could join the Beverley Road, cross the Wolds and make for Eppleworth. It wasn't to be.

The journey was fine until we got to Raywell. At the left fork that would take us down to Eppleworth and on into Cottingham was the ominous sign ROAD CLOSED. So instead we carried on to Great Gutter Lane, intending to join the A164. To our dismay, we found ourselves staring at yet another ROAD CLOSED sign. The A164 was shut, deserted, a ghost road. The awful possibility dawned on us that Cottingham might be cut off from all traffic coming from the west. How on earth were we to get home that night? The desire to sleep in your own bed is a powerful motivator. We ignored the sign, hoping that the emergency had passed, and drove onto the A164, which appeared to be completely dry. It was an eerie experience. The street lights were blazing onto an empty road. The only cars we saw were abandoned ones, littered at the side of the road at odd angles, especially at the Willerby roundabout and at the top of Castle Hill.

We drove down an equally dry Castle Road into Southwood Road and then Baynard Avenue. Almost there! But turning into West End Road at the Fair Maid we couldn't believe our eyes as another ROAD CLOSED sign barred our way. A 4x4 had appeared from nowhere, the first moving vehicle we'd seen since North Cave. It was just ahead of us, so we followed it, skirting the

Abandoned cars at the Castle Hill roundabout around midnight on June 25. (Stuart Walter)

sign, and saw Dene Road swimming in water. Rounding the corner we discovered why West End Road had been closed. There was a torrent of water rushing across it from Eppleworth Road. There was our house, just the other side of this new river, which the 4x4 had calmly sped through. Our urge to get home was stronger than ever, but the water looked too deep for us.

Looking north up George Street from Crescent Street (west), around midnight of June 25. (Stuart Walter)

We turned round and went down Hallgate. We rightly guessed that George Street would be impassable — yes, there was the river pouring through Crescent Street — but surely King Street would be O.K? Our hearts sank as we turned the corner at the traffic lights to see another torrent, or rather the same one, swirling across King Street down into the Clinic and beyond. To our surprise the same 4x4 suddenly appeared from the opposite direction, and gaily splashed its way through the torrent and past us. Driving up to the water, we stopped and tried to guess how deep it was. Shallower than West End Road? Not sure. Shall we try New Village Road?

At this point, good sense deserted us. We should have retraced our route, back to the A164, and come down into Cottingham via Harland Way. But we didn't think of it. We'd been travelling since nine that morning (eight o'clock British time) and it was now almost midnight. Weary and desperate to get home and to bed, we couldn't summon the energy to think our way round any more obstacles. So Katrin engaged second gear and cautiously pushed into the river. At mid-point the engine faltered alarmingly. Quick, first gear! More acceleration! The engine died, then stirred to life again and we were through. It was a daft risk to have taken, but two minutes later we were in our own drive. It was wonderful to find our house was dry and we were safely home. Only a few houses away the Eppleworth Road river had inundated our neighbours' properties, and it didn't bear thinking about.

Next morning we walked into the village to buy milk for breakfast and food for lunch and dinner. The river had vanished but there were brown tide marks on walls, bushes and trees. Everyone we met had a story to tell of the rain and the flooding and people being evacuated. We got home again about three hours later, and we had lunch instead of breakfast. In the afternoon I had to see the osteopath in Hull Road and Katrin wanted to go to the Bricknell Estate, so we drove there via New Village Road. We were amazed to see water streaming across the road from Thwaite Lake, and realised that Endyke Lane must have been badly affected, too.

June 26, afternoon. Thwaite Lake flooding across New Village Road, by the entrance to Boardside Walk. (Katrin McClure)

Not only that, but Croxby Primary School was sitting in and under its own lake, as Katrin discovered later that afternoon. That was not all, of course. As the days and weeks went by, the true extent and awfulness of the flooding across Cottingham, especially for houses near the becks, gradually became known to us. Even as I write this, nine months later [March 2008], we have neighbours in West End Road and Eppleworth Road who have only just got their houses restored and others who are still in caravans or living elsewhere.

June 26, afternoon. Three views of Croxby School under water. (Katrin McClure)

PART TWO

PERSONAL EXPERIENCES

2. West Cottingham

There was a great deal of flooding in this part of Cottingham, especially in the vicinity of Eppleworth Road. The sequence of photographs and stories is circular, starting at the west end of Eppleworth Road and moving eastward, taking in the northern ends of adjacent roads — Green Lane, The Dales, Sancton Close, Stewart Garth, St Margaret's Avenue, Rydal Grove, The Ridings, Dene Road (including The Dene itself) and Westfield Close. At West End Road, the sequence goes south via Baynard Avenue to Southwood Road (including Southwood Drive) and then returns westward up to Willerby Low Road, Canada Drive (also St Lawrence Avenue) and finally the Green Lane area again (south end, represented by photographs from Arras Drive).

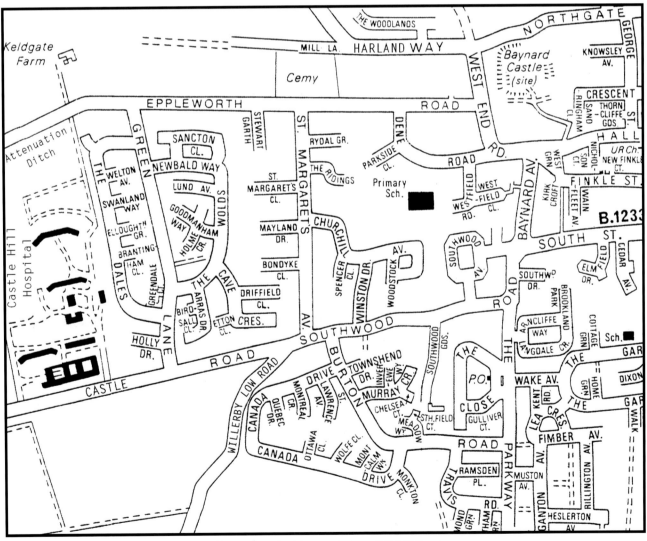

(Reproduced with permission of C J Utting.)

Eppleworth Road (West)

The west end of Eppleworth Road looking west. Notice the water spilling across the road from the culvert at the entrance to Keldgate Farm (right). It was this water that inundated the bungalows on the south side of the road. (Peter Beal)

A bungalow on the south side of Eppleworth Road (west).

25 June, 5 p.m. *Water pouring down the drive. (John Dyet)*   *A month later, clearing out the damage. (Katrin McClure)*

Engulfed

Ann Spence

Our anticipation of the flood began on Sunday 24th June when, with the help of our son and grandson, the smallest items of furniture, e.g. dining chairs, occasional tables, etc., were taken upstairs. Unfortunately my husband Bob was unable to help as his right leg was, and still is, encased in a metal frame from ankle to mid-thigh. As you can imagine, this makes movement up and down stairs difficult!

The morning of the 25th now seems somewhat blurred. We waited and watched as the water rose in the back garden. Our neighbours kept calling to see how we fared, and at one point a very kind gentleman came and lifted two easy chairs onto the sofa out of harm's way. He also dismantled the TV and the hi-fi. He came back later with a friend demanding our car keys (!) to enable them to take away the cars to a safe place on higher ground. Incidentally, our next door neighbour's car was in the garage and it was a write-off!

At about 10.30 a friend living across the road came over to chat to Bob. At about 12.00 we suggested he returned — only just in time! He was a sick man, and we watched with bated breath as he staggered across the already flooded road in wellies rather too large for him! I think it was around this time I tried to inform the emergency services of our plight — it seemed a good idea at the time. The young lady who answered my call was very patient and kept me occupied. I don't know what I expected, probably that the fire engine would take away the water!

As the clock ticked towards one o'clock we were warned by a friend that a wall of water would reach us in about twenty minutes. We had watched the water creep up the outside wall and knew when it reached the airbricks we would be engulfed. The friend was right. Water was soon creeping up the skirting board and in through the back doors! The garage (situated behind the kitchen) was engulfed, drowning the washing machine, fridge-freezer and many smaller items which were stored there.

Some of the power points downstairs were affected, but we could still use the kettle and the gas hob. Eventually the telephone was cut off (for two weeks!). People were ringing and the voice mail was working,

Looking west from Green Lane into the north end of The Dales a little after 2 p.m. BST. (John Frith)

but no-one understood we could not reply. I really didn't realise what a life-saver the telephone is. I even had to learn how to use my mobile — not an easy task! At about 4 p.m. a kindly fire officer appeared at the door to ask how we were faring. We assured him we could cope in spite of Bob's problem. By then the flood waters had surrounded the house.

Unfortunately, by mid-afternoon, when the motorists were struggling home, the swirling waters down Green Lane (meeting those coming down The Dales <u>and</u> the ones coming from between our house and the house next door) created a tidal wave at the entrance to our drive — quite spectacular! At one point two full bags of compost floated diagonally across our garden and finished up in a friend's garden across Green Lane! The wave was created by motorists driving too fast down the Lane, despite attempts by one brave soul to persuade them to go slower. No prize for guessing who were the worst offenders!

We were able to stay in the house for seven weeks and then spent a further six weeks at the Jarvis Hotel, Willerby (courtesy of our insurers), where we were well looked after and the food and service were excellent. Our daughter Louise, who lives in Durham, took on the insurance company, who fell into her hands when they said there were no builders available here. She suggested we should have an out-of-town builder, who had just done major alterations to her house in Durham, and we were allowed to employ them. We returned to our house in October which was a great relief, although we were short of furniture and carpets, etc. It was

A 'tidal wave' at the entrance to Ann and Bob Spence's drive in The Dales. (John Dyet)

mid-January before everything arrived. The builder had done an admirable job with his team of two. We were rebuilt, plastered and decorated. There are some things which I would have liked to have been done differently but I can live with them.

Waiting for the flood to strike was a very difficult time. Strangely, once it arrived I had a feeling of relief — at least it wasn't above two inches deep (in the house!), we couldn't see any sewage and we could escape upstairs!

The greatest impact of the experience as far as I am concerned was emotional. We came home but it wasn't home, and still isn't months later. I no longer have the security which home means. When it rains and blows I lie awake at night, hoping it will soon stop, wondering when the next flood will come — a prospect which we were assured would happen at a meeting of the Cottingham Flood Action Group I attended last week (April 11).

I would like to conclude by saying how kind and considerate so many people have been, many of whom we had little contact with previously. We have made new friends, and old friends have washed for us (I can tell you who is the best wash person in the area!) and entertained us in their homes. Our two cleaning girls, Vicky and Susie, organised me when I was dithering, not knowing where to start. The dust and mess had to be seen to be believed. Some items are still in cupboards upstairs!

However, we are still here in our posh new house, and my husband is having his metal, etc. removed from his leg in two weeks — just when we have almost completed the restoration! Just like a man!

Green Lane looking north just after 2 p.m. DST, showing the flooded junction with The Dales. (John Frith, John Dyet)

Coming Home to a Near Miss

Joan and Leo Murphy

At the time of the flooding we were on holiday, experiencing a heat-wave in Corfu. My daily telephone calls to my mother, who lives in the centre of Cottingham, had not prepared me for the damage which had been suffered by our near neighbours. Our garden showed that the deluge had flowed down the lawn and through flower beds, bringing soil and debris which piled up close to the house. Fortunately for us, our land slopes downwards towards the road and the water found its way around the sides of the house and onto the road, which, according to our friends, had become a river.

Two views of The Dales (north end) from the safety of an upstairs window. (Andrew Brett)

The houses on the opposite side of The Dales from us back on to those on Eppleworth Road and these were unfortunate enough to have water coming from every direction, causing enormous damage to homes and gardens. After almost a year some people have nothing but a house which is an empty shell, and they have not much hope of returning for some months.

As the flood recedes, water pours back out of an airbrick. Notice the high water mark two bricks (6 inches) above. (Andrew Brett)

We felt great sympathy for our friends who had felt fear and anxiety when so many of their possessions were lost or, at best, put into storage for months. Weeks of back-breaking gardening and carefully selected plants were also lost and we heard many hair-raising individual stories.

What could we do to help?

Regularly emptying the water containers when the dryers were installed was one of the few jobs which we were able to do, apart from offering cups of tea and the odd beer. Eventually, after admiring

Front gardens in The Dales (north end) swimming in water. (Andrew Brett)

the courage and stoicism of our friends and neighbours we decided that our only contribution to their welfare was to give a party. Our invitations were accepted and one afternoon at the end of July we got together, the lucky and the unlucky, and had a few hours of fun.

Green Lane (north)

Green Lane near the junction with Eppleworth Road. (John Dyet)

Green Lane looking north to Eppleworth Road. Junction with The Dales to the left. (Geraldine Mathieson)

Eppleworth Road (west)

Just east of the junction with Green Lane is Bryon Caley's house in Eppleworth Road. He remembers that at about 11 a.m. on June 25 a 'mini sunami' of water six inches deep surged down Eppleworth Road, swamping the houses on the south side in seconds. He and his wife spent the rest of the morning rescuing what they could. Later in the afternoon (after 3 p.m.) he started to take photographs. For another year they lived partly upstairs and partly in a small caravan bought through the insurance.

The driveway of the Caley's house. (Bryon Caley)

This is the view looking east during the afternoon of June 25. (Bryon Caley)

The house under water. (Peter Beal)

This photo shows the power of the water as it swept across the front gardens. (Peter Beal)

A wheelie bin and a dustbin floating down the side passages. (Bryon Caley)

The back garden of the Caley's house. (Bryon Caley)

The sitting room under water on the afternoon of June 25, with a view into the lake in the garden, rain still falling. (Peter Beal)

Inside the house the downstairs toilet is swimming in water. (Peter Beal)

Next day the water had all gone, but you could see the high water mark fourteen inches above ground level, well over the airbricks. (Peter Beal)

11 August 2007. *The Council refuse lorry comes to pick up damaged goods from the Caley's house ... (James Caley)*

... A settee is heaved into the jaws of the refuse lorry. (James Caley)

16 August 2007. *The floors have been stripped out ... (James Caley)*

... and the 'site safety' notices put up. (James Caley)

25 June 2008. *The aptly named 'RIVERSIDE' skip seems to tell the story. The Caley's insurers having sacked the first lot of builders, renovation of the ground floor rooms had to start all over again. Exactly a year after the flood the Caleys were still using a small caravan in the front drive as kitchen and sitting room. (Peter McClure)*

A Devastating Experience

Justine Hunt

On 25th June 2007 our home in Eppleworth Road, Cottingham was flooded. Water invaded the property from the west of Eppleworth Road and from the land to the south of the house. It resulted in two foot of water in the garage and garden and

A view of the Hunt's house and caravan, at about 2.30 p.m., with water pouring down the snicket into Sancton Close. (Geraldine Mathieson)

Eppleworth Road looking west from Justine and Roger Hunt's house. (Roger Hunt)

Ankle-deep water in the conservatory. (Roger Hunt)

Justine and Roger Hunt's house under two feet of water. (Roger Hunt)

ankle-deep water in the ground floor of the house. My husband, Roger, and I were initially marooned in the upstairs of the house but by early evening of the same day we were able to wade out to the roadside. The water receded overnight, leaving us with a devastating clear-up operation the next day. All the contents of the downstairs were ruined by water and the washer and freezer in the garage were unsafe to use as well as numerous other items. We were instructed by our insurance company to throw out all furniture and appliances

Roger Hunt with some of the damaged house contents. (Roger Hunt)

that were flood-damaged except oak furniture which could be renovated.

The Council removed heavy furniture such as settees and electrical goods. A skip was used to throw away other items. In July the insurance company sent a team of workmen to remove all the downstairs flooring and floorboards and install a number of dehumidifiers to dry out the house.

Contractors ripping up the lounge floor. (Roger Hunt)

The kitchen floor joists. (Roger Hunt)

By this time we had decided to live in our own touring caravan on the driveway, sleeping in the upstairs bedrooms at night. These seemed the best option for us as we have a large dog and were reluctant to put him in kennels. Also, we thought we would be back into the house before the winter —how wrong we were!

A drying certificate was issued early in September and then the long wait began. We were in constant touch with the insurance company and our loss adjuster but numerous delays allowed time to pass. In October we wrote to the managing director of the insurance company to say we were dissatisfied with the lack of progress, only to be told we had been 'lost in the system'. Further delays occurred, involving disagreements with the insurance company over the renovations, until finally work began on the property in mid-February 2008.

We experienced a very cold winter in the caravan. Our mental and physical health was at risk but we were well supported by friends who welcomed us into their homes and gave us meals and warmth. We felt extremely stressed with the number of telephone calls, e-mails and letters needed to resolve matters. Official help from the Council or health agencies has not been forthcoming. We have had to rely on our own ability to cope with the situation. Six months after the flood we were offered support from the Churches in Cottingham for which we are very grateful. After seven months we received a gift of light bulbs and a carbon monoxide monitor from Real Aid to help towards our new build.

A skip piled with the remains of the lounge and kitchen flooring. (Roger Hunt)

To date (mid-February), we expect to be able to move back into our home at the end of May. It has been a devastating experience which has certainly taken a year out of our lives. Our social, emotional and physical lives have been greatly challenged. In future we would like to see a structured programme of help available to flood victims. The Council and social and health agencies need to develop a 'recognised response' if flooding should occur again. Furthermore, time and money needs to be spent ensuring that the chances of flooding happening again are reduced in this area.

Postscript: Justine and Roger moved out of the caravan in June 2008. In fact it was on the 25th, exactly one year after their house was flooded, that the settee arrived in their newly decorated and carpeted lounge, and Justine could curl up in front of the TV in her own home for the first time since the day of the flood.

Contractors' vans surround the Hunt's touring caravan, where they lived for nearly a year, experiencing a very cold winter. (Roger Hunt)

Sancton Close

Water swirling down the snicket from Eppleworth Road towards Sancton Close just after 2 p.m. BST. (John Frith)

A view of the Sancton Close end of the snicket at 7.10 p.m. BST. (John Frith)

Water under the floor of a bungalow in Sancton Close at 7 p.m. BST. (John Frith)

The same bungalow in Sancton Close at 7.12 p.m. BST. (John Frith)

Water running out of an airbrick at 7.10 p.m. BST. Notice the high water mark one course above the airbrick. (John Frith)

Eppleworth Road (west)

South side of Eppleworth Road swamped with water at just after 7.15 p.m. BST. (John Frith)

Like so many houses on the south side of Eppleworth Road these were sitting in a tide of muddy water at 7.20 p.m. BST. (John Frith)

Eppleworth Road, looking west at about 7.20 p.m. BST from the East Riding's Learning Resource Centre (right). Notice how the water runs across the road to the south side where the lowest part of the valley is. (John Frith)

Eppleworth Road looking east towards Stewart Garth. (John Frith)

Stewart Garth

Stewart Garth about 7.20 p.m. from the junction with Eppleworth Road. (John Frith)

The access hatch under the stairs, water rising up to the joists. (Helen Leys)

This photo shows the power of the water pouring into a front garden in Stewart Garth during the afternoon of June 25. The house opposite was already flooded and water would soon get into the airbricks and under the floorboards at this side of the road. (Helen Leys)

St Margaret's Avenue (north)

St Margaret's Avenue at 7.23 p.m. BST, looking south from the junction with Eppleworth Road. (John Frith)

A typical scene at the north end of St Margaret's Avenue. (John Frith)

Wine, Wellies and a Good Book

Helen Bristow

Monday 25 June 2007

11.30 a.m. I was standing at an upstairs window watching my son, Robert, set off for a driving lesson. His instructor laughed when he put his wellies in the back. As I continued to look out of the window two trickles of brown water appeared either side of the road followed the gutter round the turning circle and flowed into the drain. Before too long the flow of water had increased and half an hour after setting out Robert was back as the roads were just too bad for driving. He put on his boots to get from the car to the front door. Water was still trying to go down the drain because I could see the whirlpool it created.

12.30 p.m. A little trickle of water had made its way into the kitchen and we tried hard to staunch the flow but with minimal success. We managed to lift the cooker onto the draining board, which in later days I was very glad about because we were able to cook as soon as the electricity had been switched back on two days later by our loss adjuster. I wish we'd managed to rescue the washing machine as the replacement took ages to come! By this time water was not only rushing down the road and straight down the driveway between numbers 23 and 24 but also our driveway,

A car splurges through a river of water in Rydal Grove, late evening on June 25. (Helen Bristow)

Rydal Grove from St Margaret's Avenue at 1.45 p.m. BST. (John Frith)

from front and back, and along the ten-foot and through the back gardens. The sound of the water was like a river in full spate. We switched off the electricity and moved everything from the lower shelves of the kitchen cupboards and emptied the cupboard under the stairs. (The kitchen is at a lower level than the rest of the house.) As the water continued to rise we began to fear that the whole of the ground floor would be under water so we moved some things upstairs and planned what we would move and how, if it became necessary to evacuate downstairs altogether. The men and boys enjoyed paddling and splashing about and stood in the circle debating what they should or could do. The ladies stayed inside! We had cold meat and salad for our tea and sat and read by the light of several candles while sharing a bottle of wine. Needless to say we slept well!

9.00 p.m. The water had begun to subside and when we woke up the following morning it had completely disappeared — there was not even any silt on the road.

The Ridings

St Margaret's Avenue at 1.43 p.m. BST, looking north to The Ridings (right). (John Frith)

The Ridings at 7.26 p.m. BST seen from St Margaret's Avenue. (John Frith)

Eppleworth Road (east)

The ditch on the north side of Eppleworth Road is mostly open until it becomes fully culverted near West End Road (in the far distance, out of shot). By 2 p.m. BST on June 25, shortly after this photo was taken near the cemetery, the ditch was unusually full and was already overlapping the culverts under the drives to the houses with yet more rain to come. The culverts were unable to cope and it is no surprise that many properties on this side of the road were inundated. (John Frith)

Dene Road

The north end of Dene Road at about 1.49 p.m. BST was a turbulent lake of muddy water stretching from Eppleworth Road to The Dene pond (left). The second car (silver) is stuck and being towed out by Alex Duke. (John Frith)

The Dene

The Dene is a wooded hollow lying between Eppleworth Road and Dene Road, and is a remnant of the extensive gardens of Westfield House (now the Fair Maid) before much of the land was sold off to build Dene Road in the late 1930s. The wood is still sometimes known as 'Grote's Wood' after the Grotrian family, who owned the house in the early 1900s. The hollow is marked on old maps as a fishpond, which suggests that the water table was higher in the past. Most years nowadays it is bone dry all the time, and it has long been a favourite place for children to play in. Occasionally it fills with water from an intermittent spring which, like Keldgate Spring, breaks out after prolonged rainfall has raised the water table. The Dene already had some water in it from the heavy rains of June 14 and the following week. The spring may have been active, too. On June 25 large amounts of rainwater poured into it from Dene Road and from Eppleworth Road, both over the ground and through a pipe from the Eppleworth Road (south side) culvert. The pond overflowed, flooding some nearby properties.

The warning signs were put up by the Council after The Dene filled with water in early 2001. (Peter McClure)

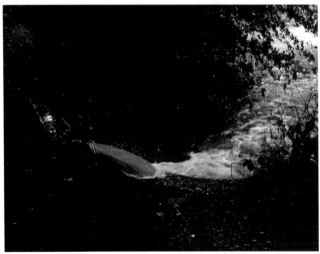

Water gushing from the Eppleworth Road pipe into The Dene at about 2 p.m. on June 25. (Geraldine Mathieson)

Water flowing from the north end of Dene Road down The Dene footpath at about 2 p.m. (Geraldine Mathieson)

The Dene footpath looking west to Dene Road at about 3.30 p.m. (Geraldine Mathieson)

Grote's Wood, The Dene pond on the afternoon of June 25. (John Horsley)

The view from 12 Eppleworth Road looking south towards Dene Wood, during the afternoon of June 25. Much of the water is from the overflowing Dene pond. Pete Featherstone recalls that the flooding was deepest about 4.30 p.m., after which the water level began to drop. (Pete Featherstone)

August 6. *A month after the flood, The Dene paths were dry but the pond was still full of water. (Katrin McClure)*

Eppleworth Road (east)

25 June, about 2 p.m. Spring water is bubbling up in front of the bush. (Geraldine Mathieson)

6 August 2007. A laden skip outside the same house. (Katrin McClure)

By 5.30 p.m. the tide of water was thigh deep. Barbara Woodward is seen wading back to her car, after checking that her aunt was safe and well. She had to climb through a window to get into and out of the house. The neighbour's car was a write-off. (David Woodward)

25 June, about 2 p.m. Plastic sheet and sandbags protecting the airbricks at front and sides of the houses. (Geraldine Mathieson)

6 August 2007. Stripping of some the houses did not start until August. (Katrin McClure)

The Junction of Eppleworth Road and West End Road

Humberside Fire Brigade van, early afternoon on June 25.
(John Horsley)

The flooded junction at 1.52 p.m. BST. (John Frith)

A similar view, shortly afterwards. (John Horsley)

West End Road looking north to the fire engine driving past
the end of Eppleworth Road. (Dave Acaster)

Saved by the Moat

Richard Lambert

The journey home from Saltend near Hedon late afternoon on 25th June was precarious due to extensive flooding, especially east of the river Hull. It was not until I turned left off Northgate into West End Road that I realised the extent of the flooding in Cottingham (*Picture 1*).

1. West End Road, looking south, late afternoon on June 25. (Richard Lambert)

2. Rising water inundating drives and front gardens in West End Road. (Richard Lambert)

The ditches along Eppleworth Road had been breached and flood water was rapidly rising at the intersection with West End Road. It was not long before the levels had risen sufficiently to inundate the front gardens and drives of the low lying houses adjacent to us (*Picture 2*).

Our house and those to the north of us are set two to three feet above the road, on what was once a rampart above Baynard Castle's outer moat, and consequently were spared the worst of the flooding.

Judging by the volumes of water filling the moat, which runs along the back of many of the houses on the east of West End Road, the local flooding could have been worse (*Picture 3*).

3. Water pouring into a neighbour's sunken back garden, once part of the outer moat of Baynard Castle. (Richard Lambert)

Certainly the moat was acting as a massive sink for much of the flood water — sadly though, not enough to save many houses from being damaged. Our shed, located in the moat, was almost submerged as the level rose to about five feet (*Picture 4*).

4. The Lambert's back garden shed is almost submerged in five feet of water.
(Richard Lambert)

The following morning the water levels had fallen sufficiently to allow us to wade out to recover the contents of the shed (*Picture 5*).

Despite having been totally submerged for over twelve hours, all of the electrical appliances stored in the shed worked without problem once thoroughly dried out. As the flood water subsided, it left a brown tide mark in the trees and hedges and a silt coating over the grass and flower beds. Many plants thrived in the aftermath, although some have since died (leylandii, and beech hedge), their roots not able to cope with long periods in waterlogged soil. It was about six to eight weeks before the final pool of standing water disappeared from the garden — we have never seen so many mosquitoes and midges.

We were fortunate; we lost a few plants and shrubs. However, as I write this (18 January 2008) many of the folk whose houses were flooded along Eppleworth Road and West End Road are still enduring life in a caravan, as work on their houses remains incomplete or, for a few, not even started.

*5. **June 26.** Richard Lambert thigh-deep in the 'moat' next morning. (Julia Lambert)*

Stress, Mess and a Change of Address!

Liz Findley

I am certain that 25 June 2007 is a date that will stay in my memory for ever. After days of heavy rain I remember standing on the patio at the back of my house looking down over our long garden, which backs onto the 'Dene Wood' area. It was mid-morning and what I encountered was an amazing sight. At the bottom of my garden, water was coming through any available gaps in the fence which divided my garden from the house to my right. However, the water was coming through with an incredible force. It was, in fact, shooting half way across the garden, resembling the jet from a fire hose. I stood for a while mesmerised by the sight. The amount of water pressure from the other side of the fence must have been immense.

My neighbour to the right was also looking out into the garden and we both expressed our concern at the amount of water collecting at the bottom of our long gardens. I remember she had to go to work at lunchtime and said to me as she left 'I'd keep an eye on that if I were you'. What did that mean, I thought, what should I do if it got worse? I felt nervous, not knowing how to react if the situation became worse.

By late morning, the water was coming up through the garden at a fast rate, now entering not only from the right (Eppleworth Road area) but from the bottom of the garden (Dene Wood). Westfield Primary School contacted me to collect my child due to the excessive water on nearby roads and the site itself. Cottingham High School sent my middle child home, too. Along with my own children I also collected a friend's two children, whose mum was unable to leave work, and with my 18-year-old son there were now six of us in the house. I kept the younger children amused with games as I anxiously looked out on to the garden as the water came nearer. I knew if the water came onto the patio area the house would definitely be under threat. By early afternoon water was collecting rapidly, filling up the front drive, too.

'By early afternoon water was collecting rapidly, filling up the front drive.' (Liz Findley)

I phoned my husband for advice. It was hard to describe the situation to him. On the second call to him, an hour later, water was starting to come onto the patio. I then asked him to come home urgently. Whilst awaiting his return, he advised me to try and block the air vents and use plastic bags and compost bags to try and stop water entering the house. Neighbours told me that the Council had been contacted and sandbags had been asked for. However, I never saw any sandbags delivered, due to the great demand generally. The children watched with excitement as one of my sons and I tried to block air vents and pile up anything available in the garage to try and stop water spreading along the patio area and into the air vents. I recall they all wanted to help, but I knew lots of soaking wet children running around would add to the mayhem so I ordered them to stay inside. The rain was very heavy, making it very difficult to achieve anything, and it was also becoming obvious that our attempts would be futile.

By the time my husband arrived in the afternoon, the situation was obviously critical. I had already got the children carrying toys and anything else they could physically carry upstairs, and tried to make a game of it seeing who could help the most, etc. We put rolled towels against the front door and back door, which of course eventually had no effect. My husband contacted my brother, who came round and helped us take any possible furniture upstairs and put the newer settee and chair on top of the older ones. We crammed as many pieces of furniture and belongings as possible upstairs and put other things on the high kitchen ledges.

Neighbours called round to each other's houses asking if any help was needed and a real 'war time community spirit' was felt. The road is one with lots of people who work all day with busy lives, which reduces the opportunities for people to get to know each other. Most neighbours generally only call hello to each other or pass a few words at the weekends whilst gardening, etc. However, this day was an exception and people really rallied round offering help. We all seem to know each other better now, having had such a traumatic experience together.

Later that afternoon the inevitable happened. Despite trying everything we could think of, water was heard sloshing around under the floor boards and eventually the carpet lifted and water started to flow in. I remember sitting on the stairs and thinking 'Well, that's it then, our fight is over'. We sat and watched the water quickly fill the rooms, and I remember a feeling of acceptance and calmness as there was nothing more that could be done.

The friend's children were collected and my 7-year-old daughter was sent to my brother's house for the night. We spent the rest of the evening looking out of the bedroom window and, finally donning shorts and Wellington boots, we all waded outside and chatted to neighbours. We discussed how much water had got in to the house, comparing times and how high it had reached. This end of West End Road was deep with water. We all knew this was dirty water, but

West End Road looking north during the afternoon of June 25. (John Garbera)

felt it necessary to walk around in it to survey the whole unreal situation and chat to our neighbours. At around 9 p.m. the rain thankfully eased. After the event we measured the dirty water level mark on my children's slide in the back garden and it was five feet high.

Amazingly traffic still tried to pass along this flooded road, including double-decker buses. At first we helped cars who got into difficulty, but then we began to feel annoyed

A closer view, looking north, of the junction of West End Road and Eppleworth Road. (John Garbera)

at the ridiculous attempts by traffic to pass through, and someone put up a makeshift 'road closed' sign. No police or fire brigade came to assist us, due to the immensity of the situation elsewhere, so we took matters into our own hands and tried to stop traffic ourselves. Large 4x4-wheel drive vehicles were particularly annoying, as many obviously were enjoying splashing through the water, returning often. However, the consequence of this was that the waves pushed more water into our houses and through low letter boxes. Eventually we shouted at traffic that tried to pass our 'road closed' signs, and if they got stuck we no longer offered help, feeling that they deserved it now. As a small canoe sailed past we stood in disbelief at this truly bizarre sight.

A fire crew ploughs through the flood on West End Road but they are on their way somewhere else. (John Garbera)

A man with a canoe or kayak having fun in the West End Road 'river'. (Dave Acaster)

The same fire engine driving in the opposite direction, making waves ... (Dave Acaster)

... followed by a police car, passing a temporary 'ROAD CLOSED' sign by Dene Road. (Dave Acaster)

Wheelie bins floating in the drives. (Liz Findley)

Wheelie bins had turned over and rubbish was floating down the street along with my newly planted flower pots. Somewhere a large collection of debris, rubbish and flower pots would end up and the children still reminisce about this, wondering where all these items eventually ended up and pitying anyone whose garden may have received this unwanted debris.

Our electricity and phone lines were soon out of action. Having nowhere to go and stay, and also feeling that somehow we should not desert our house at this time, we spent an eerie first night. In darkness, with two torches and only a wind up camping radio to listen to Radio Humberside with, we tried to cope and get some sleep. We could hear the water swirling around downstairs and the house felt dark, cold, damp and sad.

After a few hours sleep, I awoke feeling almost like it had all been a dream. I felt a dread of what the day would bring and an over whelming feeling of uncertainty. I rushed to the window and looked out. I couldn't believe the sight. Where had all the water gone? It was like someone had pulled the plug from the bath. I looked down the stairs and saw that the water level had receded and now sodden, dirty carpets and skirting boards remained. However, under the floor boards the stagnant water persisted. Our journey was just beginning.

The first week was total confusion. I remember naively thinking perhaps new carpets, decorating and some new furniture may be all that is needed to solve everything. How wrong I was!! We lacked any information and longed for someone to tell us what to do. As neighbours, we all pooled information from each insurance company but, as we now know, all companies act differently. It was obvious after a few days we couldn't live there indefinitely, with three children and the work that would be involved to rectify the situation. However, we were in for a shock when we realised how hard it would be to find rented accommodation. Our insurance company was unable to secure any accommodation for us and with up to nine families trying to secure any individual house to let in Cottingham, we felt worried. We initially lived upstairs in cramped conditions, with no hot water, heating, electricity or phone lines. The electricity supply was eventually fully rectified after about a week.

Thankfully, family and friends helped us and we would not have coped otherwise. They provided us with some meals, spare furniture for the rented unfurnished house and helped with our washing, reducing our trips to the launderette and having to eat out all the time. On our third night we managed to book only four of the five of us into a travel inn and enjoyed the hot shower, warmth and a TV for just one night. Some wonderful friends sent us a surprise of chocolates and wine complete with plastic wine glasses, to the inn. I felt really touched.

We eventually found a house in Beverley, as we were unable to secure one in Cottingham due to the very high demand. It was to be a long ordeal waiting to move into our rented house, which was not available until 1st August 2007. The next few weeks can only be described as a nightmare. The house was damp, smelled and furniture was crammed into every available space upstairs, until we managed to find some storage and move into our temporary home. When the driers and dehumidifiers were put in the noise was unbearable at times, causing difficulty in sleeping and headaches and nausea due to the dehydrating effects of the machines and the damp highly bacterial environment. We had two weeks relief in July when we went on holiday to France, but no real luxury as we stayed in a campsite. We found we could not switch off from the worry of what problems faced us on our return, but tried to be happy to ensure the children had this time to relax and forget our difficulties. Our 18-year-old son remained at home during this time.

After local builders stripped the house down to its 'bare bones', I remember returning from work after a long tiring day and staring at the remaining shell of the downstairs and the planks of wood on the floor left as a makeshift walkway to enable us to reach the stairway. I finally broke down and cried. I couldn't believe we would have our house back to its former state and it ever return to the warm, safe haven it once was. The children were incredibly brave and with the youngest (seven years old) stating that she only had her bed to play and sit on, due to the amount of stored furniture upstairs and complete lack of floor space. We joked that she lived on 'West End Bed' now, not West End Road.

Our move to Beverley went as planned, after moving as much as we could fit into the smaller house. We still had to leave many items upstairs at home. Having integrated appliances in our Cottingham kitchen, meant buying cheap new ones to go into the Beverley kitchen, which we sold on at the end of the lease. Thankfully, we also secured second hand items of furniture and borrowed from friends too. We soon settled into our Beverley home near to the beautiful Minster and town centre. In fact, we became quite fond of the place and felt thankful we were not in a caravan. We took advantage of the Council flood relief activity pass scheme with free visits to the local leisure centre.

The kitchen stripped to its 'bare bones'. (Liz Findley)

However, living in Beverley was in lots of ways a nuisance. Trying to maintain normality with the same schools, sports activities and Brownies, etc. meant many trips back and forth to Cottingham, often at peak traffic times. I also remember tediously spending many hours in cafés, waiting for activities to end or for school pick-up times. The travelling became quite an expense and one which we were not entitled to claim for. The middle, 12-year-old, child missed his local friends a lot and this did upset him, particularly during the school holidays. It was so much more difficult to pop round to friends' houses now.

We decided to appoint local reputable builders ourselves, which we now appreciate was a wise decision. We realised that waiting for our insurance firm to appoint one would have been a lengthy process. This in itself was stressful, as we became project managers, organising a kitchen company, decorators, fireplaces, carpet fitters and builder, to name a few. Trying to work, look after children and coordinate all of this was a big challenge. Thankfully, we chose a very good builder. The challenge was made worse by the extremely poor service from the insurance company. We had six loss adjusters in total, having to form a new relationship with each every few weeks. This led to a frustrating, stressful daily life of trying to make contact with them and sometimes trying to even locate which office our files were now being kept at, as they regularly moved around the country. The loss adjusters were difficult to track down and communicate with, and with people needing deposits and payments this led to the constant stress of trying to secure payments. Eventually we went down the complaints procedure system and this did help somewhat.

Stress affected each of us in different ways. My hair came out when I brushed it and I felt tired and emotional. Decisions over a new kitchen and furnishings seemed difficult, and I felt disinterested in what should have been the only pleasurable part of the process. The children got upset listening to the stressful events of the day, which had usually involved yet another call to the loss adjusters, and we realised we must not talk about this in front of the children anymore. Some days I felt I could not bear to talk about the flood and our repair work to friends or colleagues, and got upset if someone said 'Aren't you back home yet?' This question seemed to put more pressure on us, as it was difficult to explain to people not flooded the complexity of the situation. The drying process was lengthy and could not be rushed. It was interesting that the row of houses, all of similar structure and age, all took varying times to dry. The day we got the all clear we felt really excited that now something could be done to get us home.

We checked the house each day through the winter to see if it was secure and assess the progress. These visits I began to dread. I felt a real hatred for the house. It was dirty, unloved and sad. The house seemed to be no longer ours as workmen invaded it, and it resembled a building site, not our once lovely home. Many houses in the area were in differing stages of the re-instatement process and sometimes it almost felt like a competition to see who could get home the quickest. This I found upsetting and I tried to distance myself from other people's progress. Sometimes the drive to Beverley meant I could leave the stress of the house behind and I felt more relaxed as I drove into Beverley.

One of the main upsetting comments from people not flooded was the ever used statement 'Well, at least you'll have all new, or a new kitchen'. I didn't care about having new. In fact we saved a lot of our furniture and our kitchen was beautiful, our house recently decorated, too. I wished the clock would just turn back. I now appreciate that people could not possibly understand the upheaval and they were in a no-win situation as nothing they said consoled me.

After a busy January preparing to move back in, we finally achieved it on 30th January 2008. The builders had thankfully done a good job and it was wonderful to be back, to resume our normal life. As we cleaned the house and unpacked boxes, it started to feel a little like home. Somehow we needed to take ownership again. Friends and family were wonderful and sent 'welcome home' cards, wine, flowers and presents, which meant so much to us all. It has taken many more months to get back to normal and I can truly say, on the anniversary of the flood, my home felt ours again and we are once again enjoying life in it. I felt emotional on the anniversary day, listening on television to the stories of people still not back in their homes. I can also empathise with the anxiety felt by people during any periods of heavy rain, but this inner anxiety is now reducing for me. In comparison to some other families, in particular the elderly, I fully appreciate that we did not have as difficult a time. However, I hope this experience has led us to appreciate our home and life more and perhaps not take things for granted, as we all do. [2 July 2008]

West End Road on 25 June 2007. (Mike Fee)   *A similar view at the beginning of August, when skips and caravans told a story of devastation. (Katrin McClure)*

West End Road at Dene Road Junction

*West End Road, looking north, with dustbin.
(John Garbera)*

West End Road with Dene Road (left). (Leslie Chicken)

Panoramic view of West End Road from Dene Road. (John Garbera)

*West End Road, looking east towards Hallgate from the end of the
Westfield House (Fair Maid) wall. (John Garbera)*

The Castle Hill Surge

David Taylor

We live on the west side of Westfield Road and on June 25th, 2007, suffered heavy flooding in the garden. As well as the general water flowing down eastwards from the Castle Hill/Eppleworth Road area, we were surprised to observe it appearing on the ground at the end of the rear garden; we had no idea that springs were possibly situated near our land.

Between two thirty and three o'clock in the afternoon I was travelling up to Castle Hill Hospital. It had rained heavily all morning and was pouring down, and the traffic outbound was moving so slowly that it was almost stationary. As I neared the first entrance, a sudden huge powerful gush of water and gravel flooded out of the drive of a property on the northern side, a pet-supplies premises. This turned eastwards and was dispersed and slowed, mixing in with the flow already running down the road. An hour or so later, as I left the hospital, I noticed maintenance personnel pumping floodwater out of a ward block. Traffic was lighter on the return journey, but as Green Lane descended into a dip it was awash like a lake, and totally impassable.

I recounted this tale to my wife, Margaret, on returning home and thought little more about it. However, it was not long before she noticed a little water at the end of our garden, which is near to the school playing field. Investigation revealed little rivulets appearing on the surface near the perimeter of our land, and water seeping in from the direction of the field. This was making the garden soggy but was not threatening. But soon afterwards she observed that it had suddenly increased in depth and was rapidly covering the patio, eventually to about nine inches, and was turning into serious flooding around the property. We quickly realised that we had to 'do something!' We opened the gate to allow the water to escape down the drive, and it surged out on to the road, joining the water already flowing down quite quickly. But even this was insufficient reduction in depth to protect the airbricks and we had to work as a

Margaret Taylor with the brush she used to steer the water away from the house airbrick and down the drive. (David Taylor)

Wellington-booted team, my wife brushing furiously to steer the flow on to the drive, and me forcing it along, down away from the house and out onto the road.

During this time I noticed a further secondary fierce surge appear from the front drive of a property in Dene Road, and this joined the torrent flowing past, before, strangely, accurately turning right into Westfield Road and then left into Westfield

A torrent of water flowing down Dene Road and into Westfield Road (foreground). (Alan Hindley)

Westfield Road looking south from the Taylor's house towards Westfield Close. (Alan Hindley)

Close before disappearing somewhere under or around Baynard Avenue. It was two to three hours before the level dropped a bit and we were able to relax our vigilance.

By six o'clock the next morning all the water had disappeared. The surface of Westfield Road was dry, and all that remained was a waterlogged garden, and debris and aggregate in the roadway. The latter was swept up by an enormous council vehicle, which trundled by at about eleven o'clock. We also had a few photographs as a record — the phenomenon came and went so suddenly.

Fortunately we were in the house at the danger time and were able to take protective action. Certainly the airbricks would have been flooded and possibly water could have accessed the house; it was quite deep and flowing with some force. There are still some houses locally which have not yet been rendered habitable, and some of the occupants are living in caravans — several caravans remain in situ on Eppleworth Road. [January 2008]

Baynard Avenue

Several houses on the west side of Baynard Avenue were flooded on June 25. This photo shows one of the back gardens. (John Hewgill)

Christmas in a Caravan

Pat and Barry Johnson

On June 25th we were away in London, attending a funeral when we heard about the flooding in Yorkshire. Someone there checked for us to see which areas were affected. We were worried when we were told that the M62 and A63 were closed off as that was our route to travel home that night. Pat then rang a neighbour to find out more details and was shocked to hear the neighbour say 'Your house is flooded! I sent my son-in-law round to unblock the drains, thinking that to be the cause of the flooding, only for him to return and say that the water was coming UP from the sinks not going down!' We drove home through the rain with great apprehension. We took the route over the Humber Bridge as the M62 was still closed, and as we reached the Ketch in Willerby we found seven cars already abandoned along the roadside.

Southwood Road at about 2 p.m. on June 25, with water pouring off the road down into the drives below. The traffic is already being delayed by the flood water. (Hedley Brookes)

As we drove down Castle Road we saw a pipe discharging copious amounts of water from the grounds of Castle Hill Hospital onto the road side. The road was awash all the way to our home on Southwood Road, but then we saw our front garden, now resembling a swimming pool (neighbours later told us they had seen goldfish swimming around in the garden!) and the house inaccessible because of the water, which would have been about a foot deep inside. The time was almost midnight, so you can imagine our feelings of shock and devastation. We set off straight away to stay with our daughter, who had travelled with us to the funeral, to her home on Leads Road, with great difficulty due to the road conditions. Fortunately her house was not affected even though many in that area were.

10.30 next morning, we returned home to find the water had almost gone; at least we could enter the house this time, only to be greeted by a scene of devastation. Stepping inside onto 'squelchy' carpets we found wet furnishings TV, video and DVD player, walls soaked with the flood water. Then in the kitchen all appliances and bottom shelves in cupboards were waterlogged, and the fridge-freezer contained frozen, dirty water. We realised the dangers of electricity and water combined so we rang an electrician we knew. He promised to come round later that same day as he was busy helping his mother, who had also been flooded. So, out of the goodness of his heart, this electrician from KS Electrical came to check our electricity supply, and find out for us which sockets were safe to use and which were not. He was very supportive at that time. The first thing was to remove the soggy carpets and put them outside; and we were to live in the house in that state for two months before using a touring caravan on the drive. During this time the insurance loss adjuster had been round, about ten days after the flood. We made a list of damaged articles and also their values, and removed damaged furnishings, etc. into a skip at the front of the house.

The main thing was to dry out the house and for this there were dryers and dehumidifiers constantly in use. It was a SLOW process, despite constant chivvying of contractors. Hopes of spending Christmas back in the house faded and, as the weather became colder, we moved into a larger caravan, which we are still using. Christmas Day was spent at our son's home. Pat couldn't bake her usual Christmas cake in the caravan oven.

The front room of the Johnson's house, stripped and being dried out with the help of a dehumidifier. (Barry Johnson)

Postscript by Dorothy Catterick

Work is slowly progressing, and floorboards were delivered on a sunny morning in January 2008, as we sat discussing their experience of the 2007 floods in Cottingham in the caravan still serving as their home. Pat says that drying the washing had been the most difficult of household chores. They dare not fix a deadline to be back in their home, and living a normal life once more.

Each time it rains, they dread the flood happening again!

Southwood Drive

Many gardens, like this one in Southwood Drive, were flooded but thankfully not the houses. (Stuart Leadley)

St Margaret's Avenue (south)

Tides of water caused by traffic were a widespread problem on June 25. Fortunately the water at the south end of St Margaret's Avenue was not deep enough to get into the houses. (Tony Hailey)

Willerby Low Road

Residents in Canada Drive called out the Fire Brigade, shown here, at 1.31 p.m. BST on June 25. Pumping water out of the overflowing dyke on Willerby Low Road to try and protect houses in Canada Drive (behind the belt of trees on the left). (John Frith)

This photo, taken on June 25, shows a pile of sandbags in Willerby Low Road dyke near the junction with Southwood Road. They were placed there by the East Riding Council on June 15, when the dyke was also high, in a vain attempt to stop the water getting into Canada Drive. The sandbags formed a dam which forced the water to spill over and down Canada Drive, both on June 15 and June 25. (Mavis Bishop)

Canada Drive

A Council sandbag lorry drives down Canada Drive at 1.35 p.m. BST.
(John Frith)

St Lawrence Avenue

St Lawrence Avenue under water at 1.36 p.m. BST. (John Frith)

Castle Road, Green Lane (south), Arras Drive, Birdsall Close

Barry and Joan Cass, who live in Cave Crescent (off The Wolds), saw 'enormous amounts of water flowing down Castle Road'. Passing across the southern end of Green Lane it then branched off into Canada Drive at the junction of Castle Road and Willerby Low Road.

There were very few reports of flood damage in the Castle Road/Green Lane area, but just how close some houses came to being flooded can be seen in these photos of Arras Drive and Birdsall Close.

Like many roads in Cottingham on June 25, Arras Drive turned into a river. (Dave Clarke)

Arras Drive at the junction with Birdsall Close. (Dave Clarke)

Birdsall Close from the footpath from Green Lane at 2.24 p.m. BST. (John Frith)

Two panoramic views of Crescent Street, looking west, and George Street, looking north. (John Garbera)

PART TWO

PERSONAL EXPERIENCES

3. Central Cottingham

Central Cottingham was where some of the most dangerous flooding occurred. The sequence starts at the west ends of Northgate (south side) and of Hallgate (north side) and follows the flow of water eastward, from Crescent Street via George Street, King Street, Hallgate School, Caukeel Lane, Broad Lane Close, Canongate, Creyke Close and Kirby Drive to Station Road and Victoria's Way.

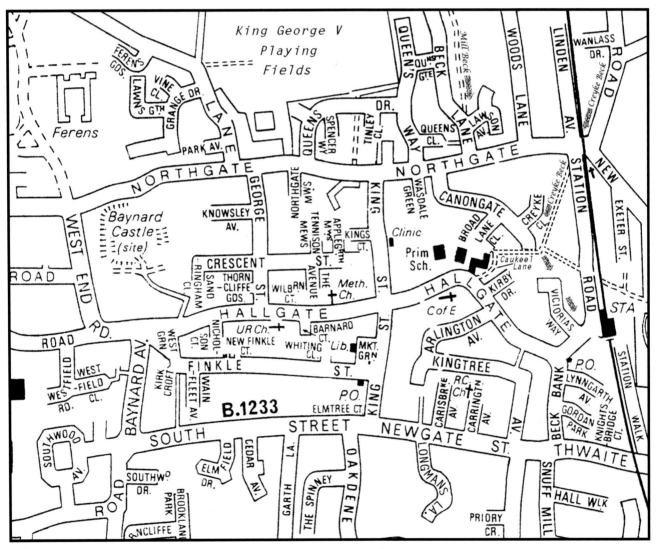

(Reproduced with permission of C J Utting.)

Northgate (west end, south side)

A car makes a bow-wave in Northgate by the entrance to The Lawns. (Steve Plater)

Traffic pushing water into driveway in Northgate. (Steve Plater)

The back gardens of some houses on the south side of Northgate drop into the old inner moat of Baynard Castle. On June 25 and for weeks afterwards the gardens became deep ponds. (Steve Plater)

West end of Hallgate, West Green

A view of Hallgate, Baynard Avenue and West End Road at 7.29 p.m. BST from an upstairs room of 278 Hallgate. There is a 'river' running through the front gardens on Hallgate. (Dave Acaster)

Hallgate, looking west into West End Road at 6.17 p.m. BST. The water is running in a river eastwards (towards the photographer). (Dave Acaster)

Hallgate, looking east from the junction with West End Road and Baynard Avenue at 7.17 p.m. BST. Water is pouring into the open ditch in front of the Hallgate houses. (Dave Acaster)

A view of Hallgate and West Green from 278 Hallgate at 7.29 p.m. BST. The open ditch is now overflowing across the driveways. (Dave Acaster)

West End of Hallgate, West Green

Surface water from Harland Way, Eppleworth Road and The Dene is culverted via West End Road to the west end of Hallgate, where it emerges in an open ditch, a good 6 feet deep and 20 feet wide, between nos. 286 and 274 Hallgate. From here the water is dyked into a larger culvert (at no. 274), which takes it north-east towards and under Crescent Street and George Street, where it reappears as Broadlane Beck in the garden of George Place. On June 25 water poured into the ditch, both from the West End Road culvert and overground from the Eppleworth Road/West End Road 'river'.

Looking east from no. 278 a little after 2 p.m., towards the culvert under the drive of no. 276. The turbulence of the deep, fast flowing water is caused by utility pipes across the ditch under the water and by the culvert itself which is hidden beneath the water. (John Horsley)

By 6.12 p.m. BST the water was up to the top of the culvert parapet but still below the driveways. (Dave Acaster)

Looking upstream at 6.12 p.m. BST towards West End Road from the driveways of nos. 278 and 280 Hallgate. This 6 feet deep ditch is normally dry or has a few inches of running water after wet weather. (Dave Acaster)

By 7.19 p.m. BST the water was surging across the driveways of nos. 280 and 278. Meanwhile the surcharged culvert at no. 274 was jetting water through to Crescent Street and blowing off the manhole covers. (Dave Acaster)

Hillcrest House, West End of Crescent Street

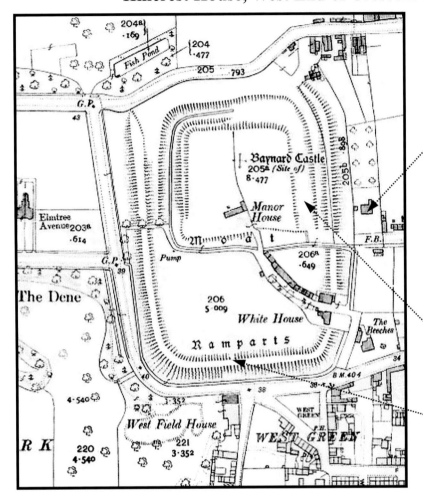

Hillcrest House

Baynard Castle site in the early 1900s before parts of the inner moat and outer moat (marked on the map as 'Ramparts') were developed as houses and gardens along Northgate, West End Road and the west end of Hallgate. (Reproduced from O.S.1910, 25", map)

Inner Moat

Outer Moat

Water rising in the normally dry castle inner moat in the garden of Hillcrest House. This section of the moat is a good 100 yards long, 15ft deep, 30ft wide at its base and up to 50ft wide across the top. (Stuart Walter)

The 'river' of water from Eppleworth Road floods across the castle site into the Hillcrest garden and .... (Chris Uney)

... flows past Hillcrest House. A three ton load of recently delivered gravel was washed away in the flood .... (Chris Uney)

... and down the driveway. Help! (Chris Uney)

Flood water starts to build up behind the gate as debris is trapped by the wire mesh attached behind the bars of the gate. (Stuart Walter)

Waterfall created by debris washed down by the flood blocking the wire mesh on the gate. (Stuart Walter)

Trying to operate the electrically powered gates and release the floodwater. The debris had to be removed before the gates could be opened. (Chris Uney)

With the gates open, the 'river' can now flow straight through the gateway and down Crescent Street .....
(Chris Uney)

... and on towards George Street. (Chris Uney)

Looking back towards the gates of Hillcrest House, at the western end of Crescent Street. The overground 'river' is now joined by underground water from Hallgate forcing its way out of the culvert manholes. (Chris Wright)

The Day my Mother Cooked Sausages!

Sue Tidder

Monday 25th June 2007 was a memorable day for lots of people — that was the day the rains came. I was at work when the rains started. I work in Pearson Park in Hull. The Park and our car park were soon under water, and our staff was busy trying to help elderly people in the locality, making sure they were safe and trying in some cases to find alternative lodgings for them. We had

Crescent Street is flooded! Submerged road sign, seat, and post box. (Chris Wright)

Broadlane Beck valley with its new 'river' running down Crescent Street and into George Street. Attempt to sandbag the open door of the white house. (Walter Shelton))

Water rising up to the level of the doors of the flats in Arnett House. Cars (left and right) blocking the road to prevent access. (Chris Wright)

the local radio on, listening to the news and trying to find out what was happening. I phoned my mother in Cottingham, to see how she was. At the time of my ringing she said there was a river running down the road!

Due to the adverse weather and the imminent flooding of our building, all staff was told to evacuate the building. I remember wading in my bare feet to my car, then putting on my socks and shoes, because of the depth of water. There was no way you could see the road — the whole of the road and park had become a vast lake. I managed to get home, despite the road conditions. No sooner had I arrived home, I got a phone call from my sister, Kate, **in France.** She had phoned my mother because she had heard about the weather on the news! My sister Kate was concerned about Mother, who is in her late 80's, so I told her I would ring again after I had been to see what was happening. My mother said the water was starting to come through the door, so I jumped in my

People wading through the flood water. Car placed earlier to block the road to traffic. (Chris Wright)

car, with loads of old towels, etc., and black bags, and made my way to mother's ground floor flat in Crescent street. I did not get very far. As I turned into George Street, I suddenly realised how bad it was, and was forced to park my car at the top of George Street and wade waist deep to get to my mother's flat at the junction of George Street and Crescent Street. This would be approximately 2.30 –3.00 p.m. and the water was already about mid-calf deep, **inside** the flat with objects floating around in the dirty water.

My first concern was 'How do I get her out?' I knew she would be unable to walk through the water as I had just done, because water was gushing up through culverts like fountains, and it was impossible to know exactly where you were walking. Neighbours wandered in and informed me that police had been informed, and soon a policeman appeared. I told my mother to sit on her bed and get out of the water, but she ignored me — and the neighbours and police. I quickly tried to grab some of her belongings to put them on top of other furniture. Neighbours also helped lift some items, but they too were trying to save their own belongings. I managed to fill a black bag with clothes, etc. and took them back to my car. I did four journeys in all, trying to save items belonging to my mother — but so much was lost.

Humber Rescue with inflatable dinghy in Crescent Street. (Mike Fee)

I phoned relatives to inform them of the situation, and told them that, according to the policeman, the fire service were on their way and possibly would get my mother out in a dinghy. There were other elderly people in a similar situation to my mother. Eventually three young firemen arrived, and carried my mother outside (much to her delight as she was chatting away non-stop) and took her to a vehicle at the Hallgate end of George Street. I, of course, was parked at the Northgate end of George Street. At this point, other emergency staff had arrived, and I told the fireman that I would take my mother back to my house, as emergency staff was trying to find places to care for these elderly people, some disabled, on a temporary basis.

My next problem was how to get to my mother home. I went down West End Road — no way could I get through. I then tried King Street — the same problem. I then went via New Village, onto Thwaite Street, and back into the centre of the village. At this point my brother had arrived, picked up my mother from the Rescue Vehicle, and was trying to take her to my house. Fortunately he spotted me and flashed me with his car lights.

We got my mother back to my house, where I quickly removed her wet clothing and rubbed her down, trying to get her warm. My mother had not eaten at this point, because she had tried to cook herself some sausages and dropped the pan in the water! My brother set off, waded through to get Mother some fish and chips, which is what she said she fancied.

She stayed the night with me, sleeping on a two-seater settee downstairs as she is unable to access the stairs, and then went to my brother's the next day, where she slept on a bed he'd brought downstairs for her. She stayed there for a couple of weeks. He too had problems with flooding, due to water coming off the sports fields down Inglemire Lane. My sister Glynis travelled up from Kent and took Mother back with her for a month, while alternative accommodation could be found for her.

The family had not realised that my mother was not insured. She had previously been insured. I guess it was oversight due to her age; as a result she had lost everything. It was heartbreaking as my sister-in-law, Heather, and I went through her personal belongings, including photographs, cards and letters, just throwing them out because they were contaminated and ruined. My brother Clive and nephew had removed some of the larger items and carpets, but it all had to be cleared as soon as the water subsided, which was the next day after the floods, but the smell was unbelievable!

As a result my mother needed new furniture, new cooker, fridge-freezer, washing machine and tumble dryer. I applied on behalf of my mother for a grant through the Local Authority and got a cheque for £500. Later, through St Mary's Church, I got another cheque for £200. By August, the Local Authority found her a ground-floor flat in Beverley. My sister Kate and I took photographs and e-mailed them to my sister Glynis in Kent. Kate and I bought carpets and curtains for the flat; also we bought various pieces of furniture for her, ready to come into her new flat. My sister Glynis also ordered bedroom furniture to be delivered there.

Easter 2008. Skip, Portaloo and temporary storage container still at corner of Crescent Street and George Street. Repair work still not completed. (Dorothy Catterick)

My mother has lived in Cottingham for over 50 years. She now struggles to get out of the house unless in a wheelchair. She is living in Beverley; she knows no-one and is unable to get out of her flat. She is becoming very lonely and depressed, and is very unsettled. Although I ring her every night, I can no longer visit her four or five times a week, as I used to do. We are now in 2008, and her original flat is still not ready for occupation. Due to what happened to her, she is not sure if she wants to move back to Cottingham. The thought of having to get carpets and curtains for Crescent Street and to go through everything again, is really upsetting her. She is getting very low and depressed, the longer she is in Beverley. For her, and lots of others, it is a very difficult situation for someone of her age. At least my mother had a family to rally round her — there are lots of elderly people who have no-one to help them.

Although Crescent Street has flooded in the past, never to the extent of 2007 — and let's hope it never does again!!

Dorothy Catterick reports that Mrs Tidder moved back into her old flat, refurbished by the Council, on March 3rd. Sue Tidder says her mother 'is a new woman!'

People coping with flooding in Crescent Street and George Street

Wading towards Arnett House in Crescent Street. Can we get that far with dry trousers? (John Caley)

Another group checking the residents of Arnett House (left, out of shot) with Humber Rescue in attendance. In the left background police are assisting an evacuee. (Chris Wright)

A family leave their house in George Street. (Chris Wright)

A cyclist wades past one of the two cars blocking George Street to traffic in an attempt to reduce the waves caused by passing vehicles. (Chris Wright)

My House in a River

John Caley

My house is in George Street, west side, at bottom of marked dip in road, roughly above a culverted watercourse (Broadlane Beck).

Monday June 25th

Rained continuously and very heavily from early morning.

08.30   Phoned client to postpone job for the day.

09.30   Knock on door, Council asking if anyone would like sandbags — took some and some for neighbour.

A few sandbags at the door of John Caley's white house. (Walter Shelton)

10.00   Still pouring, large puddles forming in road opposite house.
Positioned sandbags in doorway, also for elderly neighbour.

10.30   Covering of surface water over road.

10.45   Water seeping through floor and lower walls.
I think that it was first house to flood.
Started to carry things upstairs where possible — clock, light furniture, equipment.

11.00   An inch of water throughout house — clear rainwater.
All telephone lines engaged or blocked.
Passing cars causing extra wash, neighbours and people out, discussing and trying to help.
Family came and took things away for storage.
People were assisting one another, helping in all sorts of ways.

Water rising to cover sandbags and seep through the door. (John Caley)

11.30   Six inches water in house, paddling about, carpets and light items floating.
Water outside flowing west to east from Crescent Street area.

12.00   Ten inches of water in house, still raining hard.
About ten houses on either side now flooding.

15.00   Twelve inches in house.
People parked cars across street to form a barrier, but too late really …
Council workers helped people to carry things etc.
Still raining, other side of street, cottages flooded deeper.

Two cars parked in the flooded road to (partially) block the road to traffic. (Walter Shelton)

15.00 Water flowing quite fast like river — two feet deep in middle, about twenty feet wide. Followed natural route of former watercourse across dip in road. Police came to check which houses had been vacated and which had occupants remaining.

18.00 About two feet of water in house — abandoned — locked up and went to Mum's.

Fire and rescue services arrive to assist the police in helping stranded residents. (Chris Wright)

Next day

By 07.00 when returned to property, no sign of water — all gone …
Carpets sopping, walls and floors wet through, kitchen cupboards and equipment damaged.
Any articles unable to be moved were damaged; not sewage, only ground-water but dirty.
Plaster wet, had to be chipped off and removed; decorations ruined.
Skirting boards to be replaced.
[concrete floor, otherwise joists and floorboards to remove and replace]
Electrical system to be replaced and checked.
Contacted insurance during morning.
Took carpets and damaged goods outside, arranged for removal.
Installed fans, dehumidifiers and driers per insurance — for six weeks.
Lived upstairs with weekly allowance from insurance for food, power etc.
Lots of take-aways.

Next Day. *All the flood water has drained away. Alex Duke's car is high and dry where he parked it the previous day to prevent cars driving down George Street. (Walter Shelton)*

Since then

Gradually got house in order, but end of November before was able to move back downstairs — five months.
Everything nicely restored and replaced — not best of situations, but property enhanced, if anything — was lucky as only just moved in and planned to renovate — new carpets, decorations, appliances and electrical goods.
Noticed particularly how community spirit had been apparent. Some local properties have still not been re-occupied [January 2008].

Emergency Services:
Police, Humberside Fire and Rescue Service, Humber Rescue, Ambulance Service
Crescent Street (west)

Police assisting residents in George Street at the junction with Crescent Street. (Chris Wright)

Paramedic approaching Arnett House in Crescent Street. (Chris Wright)

Police officer with rescue vehicle in George Street. (Chris Wright)

Rescue vehicle and Humber Rescue with inflatable dinghy evacuating Bailey House flats in Crescent Street. (Chris Wright)

Police and bystanders watching the evacuation of Arnett House at the corner of Crescent Street and George Street. (Brian Goodison)

Emergency Services:
Police, Humberside Fire and Rescue Service, Humber Rescue, Ambulance Service
George Street

Police, Humber Rescue and Paramedic near White Lodge and the entrance to
George Place in George Street . (Chris Wright)

Police and the Fire and Rescue Service at the
entrance to George Place, George Street.
(Chris Wright)

Police and the Fire and Rescue Service assisting residents
(carrying bedding) to evacuate their houses.
(Chris Wright)

Policeman wading past houses on west side of George
Street. (Chris Wright)

My Home in a Skip

Christine Moffat, introduced by Dorothy Catterick

Walking down George Street on my way to the shops at the beginning of August, I was passing the area that had recently suffered very badly from the flooding of Crescent Street on June 25th. Already the builders were in evidence, with their vans and rubbish skips, and other equipment, when I saw Christine standing outside her lovely 19th-century cottage, looking 'lost and forlorn' as the workmen were removing debris out of the front door and into a skip in the garden. As I greeted her she said, 'Look at my home in a skip!' This made such an impression on me that I offered to take some photographs of it for her as she didn't think that her relatives in Scotland would believe what she told them about what had happened to her in the flooding in Cottingham. At Christmas I was able to photograph a happier Christine as she was waiting to leave her home, now restored, to go to Scotland for Christmas.

Rubbish skip, damaged gas fire etc. being cleared after the flood and placed outside the house. (Dorothy Catterick)

Her words retell the horrors of that day in June when the flood waters flowed through her home.

Outside the rain was pouring down as I was working in the back room and I looked out of my window to see that the rain did not appear to be draining away down the sinks in the courtyard, but was pooling there instead. I decided that there must be a blockage, so I took the broom handle to poke out the sinks, but to no avail, so I then telephoned a friend who came round to help and told me that the water in the street was not draining away either!

I decided to go next door to my elderly neighbour, to find her already with her 'Emergency Bag' packed ready, as she had been trained to do during her service in the armed forces during the war. I thought this was a bit drastic, but went back home. Meanwhile the Council had delivered a few sand bags, but these were of little use.

It was now about 6.15 p.m. and beginning to get darker when my other neighbour came round saying we were going to be flooded and urged me to move furniture off the floor and take things upstairs, which she helped me to do. By this time the water was mid-calf deep inside the house and beech masts and leaves were floating with other bits and pieces around the rooms. As I was upstairs sorting my

Flood water in George Street reached the front door. Police arranging rescue. (Glen Johnson)

things out, there came a very loud knocking on the front door and a loud voice saying that it was the Police and that they had come to evacuate all the area. This I had no intention of doing! Leave my house, no way! Then I heard a voice say 'We've got a difficult one here', at which I said that I wasn't but when he added that the Chief Constable, or whoever had sent them, had told them that it was because of the potential danger from gas and electricity supply damage, I had to agree and prepare to leave. They said that I would be taken out in a 'boat', which did not transpire as they required the dinghy to evacuate another neighbour across the way from George Place, more in need of rescue than I. As I watched

Earlier in the day, cars driving down George Street splashed water into the houses. (John Horsley)

through the window I saw cars driving through the flood water and causing waves to increase the water in the houses, until one gentleman drove his 4x4 across the road to block traffic off. The flashing lights of the fire engine were reflecting in the water as the Emergency Team worked to get everyone away to safety.

Soon two men with waders on came to carry me between them to the other side of Crescent Street (or The Crescent River as a friend called it!). As they progressed across they were above waist deep and I saw the water gushing like fountains up from the manholes with even the lids spinning on top of them with the force of the water.

They set me down at the other side of Crescent Street with my friend, whom I had previously phoned asking if I could come to her until the emergency was over, little thinking that it would be November before I was back home. The Emergency Team asked if I wanted to go with others to Beverley Leisure Centre. I declined and told them I'd made my own arrangements.

4x4 driven to block George Street. (Glen Johnson)

Fire and Rescue Service and Humber Rescue. (Chris Wright)

My friend took me to her home in Hallgate and soon had me dried off and wrapped in a rug, drinking hot soup...and brandy! Needless to say I slept little that night as all I could think was that people would be looting my house! So early next morning, without waiting to eat breakfast, I made my way down George Street to find that the flood water had gone and left behind rubble all across the road at the end of Crescent Street. Still apprehensive of what I'd find when I opened my front door I unlocked it and opened the door to find my pink carpet was no longer pink and that everything was soaking wet and covered with debris. In the kitchen, the cupboards, cooker, washing machine and fridge-freezer were full of dirty water.

Inspection point cover lifted by the force of the water flowing from the Broadlane Beck culvert. (This has been reported as up to 4 feet, or even 7 feet, high at times). (Chris Wright)

Next I warily tried the gas and electricity to find that they worked O.K. Standing there amidst all the devastation, all I could think was 'Where do I start?' I had never made an insurance claim before, but decided that must be the first thing to do, so I rang Zurich Insurance and asked for the Flood Department. From this point on it seemed like a labyrinth of departments, loss adjusters, surveyors, etc. and the phone bill kept growing! The insurers allocated a 'Key Worker' to take care of me and advise me what to do next, and what to claim for. Lists needed to be made of items that had been damaged, furniture, etc. that needed to be restored. And my piano, that was just full of water, had to be taken to be dried out and restored and stored until after the house was repaired. The carpet had to be taken up and put outside for the Council to collect; my gardener helped me with this task.

Easter 2008. Wet plaster and damaged gas fire removed from the house.
(Dorothy Catterick)

As it was now Sunday I decided to attend church, as was my custom, and was very glad I did, as I felt the support that I was sorely in need of. Often I was on the verge of tears, but didn't actually cry. I felt 'saturated with emotions' that I'd never experienced before. In retrospect I suppose it was the effects of shock, but because there was so much to do and supervise there wasn't time for weeping.

I had previously arranged to attend the United Reformed Church Assembly in Manchester so I went as planned. I was so glad I did as during the course of the meetings a representative from AXA Insurance Company, who had come to give a talk on 'Church Insurance', was sitting right next to me, a one in four hundred chance, and what a blessing that turned out to be! I was able to ask him all the questions that had arisen so far, about the insurance claims and the best way to deal with them, putting my mind at rest.

Until the tests on the walls, which had been stripped of plaster by the builders, showed that they were dry enough to be re-plastered, there were large blowers going all the time and windows were kept open. Each day I went to stay in the house upstairs so I could be available to urge the workmen on (make tea) and then I went back to my friend's to sleep. It was November before I actually returned home to continue organising the rest of the replacing of shelves and cupboards, etc. and the decorating.

Now when I look back it seems like quite an adventure, and also the community spirit generated amongst all those in the same predicament is marvellous. I can look at my home now all 'bright and new' and see the positive things that resulted from the 2007 Floods in George Street, while still remaining apprehensive every time it rains!

Christmas 2008. Christine Moffat at the door of her restored house. (Dorothy Catterick)

Flooding in George Street near the junction with Crescent Street

View showing the depth of the flood water. (John Caley)

Policeman checking the flooded houses. (Chris Wright)

Couple with two dogs (one being carried, one defiantly swimming) leaving the flooded area. (John Garbera)

Rescuer carrying a friend out of the flood. (John Caley)

George Place and the Boat Rescue

Alan Wright

On Sunday, June 24, 2007, the Meteorological Office issued a severe weather warning suggesting that heavy rainfall would affect our area. I checked that the part of Broadlane Beck, which runs through part of my garden, was reasonably clear of debris. The beck normally runs for only a few days each year, but when it does it brings down plastic bottles, cans, takeaway containers, etc., which I have to clear from my boundary fence.

September 2007. Early 19th-cent. brick culvert, where Broadlane Beck enters the garden of George Place. (Peter Kerr)

It was raining heavily on the morning of the 25th of June, but we had booked our two little dogs in for a trim and had to take them to the pet shop in Hessle. At about 9.30 a.m., water was already overflowing from the sinks in Prestongate. We returned home to find water flooding George Street and my wife telephoned the East Riding of Yorkshire Council to ask if someone could come to clear the sinks which had been blocked for some considerable time. During the morning she continued to telephone the Council, Yorkshire Water and the Environment Agency but with no success. As the water continued to rise, my wife telephoned the Council and the police to ask if George Street could be closed to traffic. Vehicles were driving rapidly through the flood and creating bow waves so that water was washing into the cottages and down my drive. The Council said it was the responsibility of the police – the police said it was the responsibility of the Council! Eventually the residents blocked the street with their own vehicles.

At 1.00 p.m. we telephoned the pet shop to see if the dogs were ready to collect. Unfortunately, the shop had been flooded and they had been unable to trim the dogs. We set off to collect them and bring them back home. After nearly three hours of driving along flooded roads, being stuck in traffic jams and finding many roads closed, we had to return empty handed and leave the dogs at the pet shop.

Water flowing down Crescent Street and into George Street. Sandbags at the entrance to George Place (between the trees in the centre of the picture). (Walter Shelton)

On our return to George Place, the situation was becoming very serious. Water was pouring down the drive, so I decided to leave my car in the street. I managed to acquire a few sandbags from a neighbour and tried to form a barrier at the end of my drive – this proved to be futile. I also tried to block up the air-bricks but even at this stage, I did not

The water reaches the drive to George Place (between the trees on the left of the picture). (John Garbera)

really believe that the house was in danger of being flooded. Fortunately, my wife was more pessimistic and began moving some things upstairs, the first being our daughter's work for her university dissertation, which she had left with us for safe keeping while she was in Africa. Items were also being put on tables, chairs, worktops, windowsills downstairs, just in case.

Water then entered the garage and I tried elevating as much as I could but did not know at that time how severe the flooding would be. By teatime, the flow of water had turned into a torrent and I had to retreat inside. Water was already coming into the house. It had come through the floorboards with a gush. A neighbour's fence panels were ripped off by the forceful water, which was now entering our garden from all the surrounding properties. We were completely engulfed.

The fridge-freezer, full of food, toppled over and was floating around in the kitchen and a tall bookcase in the dining room had fallen onto the table. Chairs, sofas, lamps and cheque books were bobbing up and down in the dirty water. One does not get a chance to rehearse for such an event and we did not manage to save many of our valued possessions in time. We lost a large collection of books, family photographs, records, etc., many of which are irreplaceable.

By 7.30 p.m. we had moved upstairs and the house was completely surrounded by a sea of muddy water. Downstairs, it had flooded to a depth of

Police and firemen at gateway to George Place. (Chris Wright)

three foot. The garage, sheds, greenhouse, two cars and our caravan were all flooded and the contents scattered about. At the lowest point in the garden, only the tops of the rose arches were visible and they were six foot high. We dialled 999, but soon after our phone went dead and even the mobile telephone stopped working because it was wet.

We were just feeling cut off from the rest of the world when I noticed a police officer in George Street. My wife opened the window and called out for help. He waded part way down the drive but had to retreat because there was a strong possibility that he would be swept off his feet. He shouted to us to stay where we were and he would get a boat. We told him to rescue our elderly neighbours first.

Humber Rescue arrive and launch inflatable dinghy. (Chris Wright)

About half an hour later, we were delighted to see a crew from Humber Rescue arriving with an inflatable. They waded down the drive almost waist deep and were roped together with the rope fastened to the concrete fence posts. The boat came to the back door of the house and we had some difficulty scrambling into it because it was quite high up with the depth of the water. We were taken into George Street carrying a few spare clothes and an empty dog bed. One of the neighbours thought the dogs must have perished because they normally go everywhere with us. A friend living nearby kindly took us in to get dried out and gave us a very welcome cup of tea.

In case anyone wonders what happened to the dogs, they were taken by the pet shop owner to her own house. At about 10 p.m. we were able to get to Hessle via Hull city centre and Clive Sullivan Way and collect two very relieved little dogs and took them to our emergency accommodation.

Although we were exhausted, neither my wife nor I could sleep that night — truly a day to remember!

Humber Rescue taking people to dry land. (Chris Wright)

***Sepember 2007.** Broadlane Beck leaves the garden of George Place. Debris of branches and rubbish . (Peter Kerr)*

The next day, when we returned to Cottingham, we were amazed to find that the water had gone, leaving a residue of silt. The garden was a muddy grey colour and was full of mysterious objects, In the beck were tons of gravel from various drives and there was a wheelie bin, two large bags of compost, our own garden seat, several watering cans, a can of used oil, a football, some planters, not to mention a mountain of bottles, cans, fence panels, leaves and branches.

The force of the water coming through our property was quite awesome. I pray that it never happens again.

Nightfall on June 25 in George Street and Crescent Street

George Street looking south as the daylight fades. (Ros Wareham)

A view of Arnett House, Crescent Street, after dark.
(Stuart Walter)

Repair work at White Lodge, George Street, in March 2008

Bulk delivery of sand.
(Dorothy Catterick)

Site safety notice on the front door and a delivery of aggregate.
(Dorothy Catterick)

An Unexpected Day at Home

Julian Savory

My house is on King Street near the junction with Northgate. On the Monday morning I was due to take a number of piano lessons at Hull Collegiate School at Tranby Croft, Anlaby. It was raining exceptionally heavily and although I competently cycle in most weathers, it seemed so heavy and prolonged that I decided to ring for a taxi. The taxi driver commented on difficulties being encountered on his journeys, specifically that Priory Road was flooded, and the main Beverley-Hessle Road had long tailbacks of stationary traffic caused by similar difficulties near the Waitrose roundabout. The only alternative route was Eppleworth Road, so we set off in that direction.

It was still pouring with rain and as we went along little water splashes began to appear on the road, followed by puddles, then very large puddles. Shortly these became small lakes and then very large lakes, and we had not gone very far before there was an enormous lake right across the carriageway and verges. At this point the driver and I looked at one another and agreed that it would be wise to abandon the journey and go back to my home. I was unable to leave Cottingham in any of the directions which would take me to Anlaby.

When I got home I telephoned the school secretary's office to explain why I hadn't arrived, and to warn them that they should be aware that the flooding seemed to be escalating and that perhaps they should consider closing. The person answering thanked me but said they were fine, there was no problem anywhere in the vicinity. However, difficulties did develop, as during the day flooding affected their area, too, and I understand that there was considerable disruption and a few pupils were unable to reach their homes until ten o'clock at night.

So I was at home, and as the morning went on all the day's engagements were cancelled either by me or by the other party as conditions continued to worsen. It was pouring with rain and I didn't venture out again. I really should have enjoyed this day of unexpected leisure, but I felt very uneasy and unsettled. It was a strange situation and everyone was a bit disconcerted and alarmed. There seemed to be water all over the place, and in the late evening I looked out from an upper window and saw that the school playing fields and the Clinic car park were partially flooded under a lot of water, more than I had ever seen before. I found it a bit disturbing but I went to bed and thought no more about it.

Cottingham Clinic, King Street, with the car park under water from Broadlane Beck overflowing. (Ros Wareham)

In the morning the water had gone, but I subsequently discovered that the Clinic had been flooded and the water had extended right across King Street like a lake and into the cottages opposite. There is a bit of a dip in the road at that point and, whilst I was unaware of it, there had been quite deep flooding there, only a little further down the street from where I live.

The thing that struck me was that no-one really knew what to do. The circumstances were unprecedented, and nobody had encountered such a situation on this scale in Cottingham within living memory. I think that should something similar happen again, residents, the emergency services and the Council might be able to respond more effectively with the benefit of their experiences in June.

Flood water on the King's Court access road draining into the Broadlane Beck. (John Horsley)

King Street inundated by Broadlane Beck with King's Court on the right and Hallgate school's entrance opposite. (Ros Wareham)

This article by Liam Potter, a Year Five pupil at Hallgate Junior School in 2007, has been adapted and reprinted with permission from the school newsletter produced by the Journalism Club with the help of Miss Julie Osgerby.

Volume I, Issue 4   July 2007   HALLGATE

Primary Post

The Ferocious Flood by Liam Potter

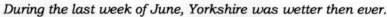

During the last week of June, Yorkshire was wetter then ever.

The benches and the play area at 5 p.m. on 25 June. (Julie Osgerby)

Water was overflowing on the streets, towns and schools causing havoc and misfortune and our school playground was completely covered in what looked like an ocean (the water even covered the picnic benches!) However the Victorian building stood tall without a drop of water inside.

Although no water got in our school, some homes in Hull and Cottingham were so badly flooded that people living inside had to be evacuated by firemen.

Broadcasters all over the country were talking about a man in Hessle, who had died in a drain all because of rain and other terrible things that had consequently happened because of the Floods.

On the Monday of the flood, the Year 5 children were taking part in Peer Mediation training, the second part which had to be cancelled along with all other lessons as the rain that had been pouring all night showed no sign of stopping by dinner time. The Beck's banks burst, and Mr Lloyd made the decision to close the school, ringing all of the children's parents to collect them for health and safety reasons due to the weather.

Overflow from Broadlane Beck in King Street (left to right) and Mill Beck in the trees on the right (top to bottom) meet and flood the school field.
(Julie Osgerby)

Everybody was extremely excited, as they sat in Hall A watching a DVD with all of their belongings, waiting for their parents to arrive. Similar things happened in the Infants school, which fortunately also remained dry.

The schools remained closed on the Tuesday but everyone was back to normal by Wednesday. Most other schools were the same but Croxby Primary School children have been extremely unfortunate. The flood water took over their school and it is being closed until September!

We weren't completely unaffected, however. Mr. Chadwick must have been disappointed when the Athletics Club event at Costello stadium, against many other schools in the East Riding, was cancelled due to the conditions. As well as this, the Year 3 Sculpture Park visit, that should have happened on the day of the flood, had to be postponed.

All of the hard working people who were trying to help with the Summer Fair and those who were hoping to arrive were disappointedly told that it was cancelled because the field was totally waterlogged. Who would have thought that a flood could cancel this much?

We weren't the only ones to suffer though. In the streets, cars were literally floating around speedily in the mad, invading water, and people were actually swimming in this just to prove how big a commotion there was.

Many people were taking photos like mad as nobody in the whole

Steps and access ramp at the rear of the 1892 building.
(Julie Osgerby).

East Riding had ever seen anything quite like this. Councillors all over the country are putting millions of pounds into fixing people's lives and schools. Hopefully nothing close to this will ever happen again.

A week before term ended, there was still a massive puddle by the Year 4 and 5 entrance.

A Serious and Very Frightening Experience

Harold Mankel

My wife and I have always liked Cottingham and was looking forward to settling down here for the rest of our lives. We never thought that one day we would be flooded out. This should never have happened if the authorities had cleaned out the dykes more often than they do. We were watching the dyke rise, never thinking that it was going to rise over the banks, but sure enough it did. We have had heavy rain before, since we came here, but this was different. It caught us by surprise and we could do nothing about it. We wondered if the water would ever stop rising. There was torrential water coming down the beck. I've never seen anything like it. This was serious and very frightening.

The deepest water in Hallgate School playing field was adjacent to Mill Beck (behind the metal palings). Broad Lane Close properties are in the background. (Mike Fee)

It was about six o'clock in the afternoon when the water started to come in the house. The back bedroom and the conservatory was four or five inches deep in water. They were extensions that we built at a lower level than the rest of the house. When it came really heavy two of my grandsons and my in-laws came down to help. We are next to the bridge that goes over the beck along the back lane by the school (Caukeel Lane). It was the boarding on the side of the bridge (to stop the kids falling into the beck) that was stopping the water flowing through, so it was coming back and into our home. So they broke a hole in the boarding to let the water through. The force of the water when it came through threw them back. The water in the house subsided but the damage was done.

Caukeel Lane snicket at about 2 p.m. looking towards Hallgate with rain water running down and meeting flood water spilling from Mill Beck. (John Horsley)

Caukeel Lane snicket, early in the afternoon of June 25, looking towards the footbridge and Broad Lane Close showing the extent and depth of the overflow from Mill Beck. Close inspection of the photograph shows that the boarding on the bridge (far left) is still intact. (John Horsley)

Next Day, 5 p.m. The boarding at Caukeel Lane footbridge cut away to release the build-up of water in the Mill Beck. The water level mark is indicated on the brick wall just below the graffiti. Harold Mankel's house can be seen behind the boarding. (Pat Elliott)

It was a good job we have a good family to help out. I don't know what we would have done if it hadn't been for our children helping us out, as we are in our eighties and not able to manage like we used to do. But to cut a long story short our two sons, and our Paul being a builder, has got us just about back to square one. The floor has been re-laid, we've new carpets and decoration and it's all wonderful [March 2008].

Since then we have heard all sorts of stories why it happened, and why the beck couldn't cope with all the water that was flowing in our homes. But what I do know is that, when we were young, the drains around Hull and Cottingham was looked after better than they are today. In our days the men used to go in the drains with long rubber boots, cut down all the weeds and put them into the lorry and take them away. The men here cut down the weeds but leave them to rot on the banks. Then during the winter weather they slide down into the water. Then when Spring comes they take roots, so we are back to square one, not leaving much room for the water to flow away. If the weeds was taken away like they did in the old days, we would not have this bother, but I suppose, like a lot of other things, there isn't a lot of money for the authorities to hand around. It was a big mistake to fill Cottingham Road drain in. It used to take all the water from the smaller drains, and from there it flowed into the River Hull, and then the River Humber.

Canongate

Canongate looking south with Creyke Close junction on the left. (Mike Fee)

The cul-de-sac end of Canongate which stops at the laurel bushes. (Martin Stroud)

Police came to rescue someone but then had to be towed away. (Ros Wareham)

Creyke Close

Looking up Creyke Close from Canongate. (Martin Stroud)

Looking up Creyke Close with a forlorn "TO LET" sign for one of the flats. (Martin Stroud)

The ground floors of every property in Creyke Close were flooded. (Martin Stroud)

Water just starting to get into the gardens. Looking down Creyke Close towards Canongate. (Martin Stroud)

Later in the day, gardens and ground floors flooded.

Whilst some people suffered the distress of being evacuated, others saw the funny side. (Ros Wareham)

Rear of the flats which back onto Creyke Beck.
(Martin Stroud)

Wheelie bins in their normal neat row.   *Later the same day, wheelie bins floating free.*
Rear gardens in Creyke Close with water from overflowing Creyke Beck. (Martin Stroud)

Kirby Drive

Back gardens of several houses in Kirby Drive were inundated by Mill Beck, a panoramic view. Fortunately the houses are on higher ground and escaped serious damage. In the distance are houses in Victoria's Way (left) and Hallgate (right). (Peter Conyers)

A view from Kirby Drive across to houses in Victoria's Way. (Peter Conyers)

The basement of a Kirby Drive bungalow. At the height of the flood the water was 5–6 feet deep and just failed to reach above the airbricks and damp course; the basement was flooded to the ceiling. (Peter Conyers)

A Cellar-full of Creyke Beck

Gavin Smith
Managing Director of Cottingham MOT Centre

Monday 25th June, 2007

2.00 p.m. I arrive back from Sorrento to work, gone from lovely weather to very wet. Yard at work has started to fill with water. Also Creyke Beck (behind the premises) is very high. Water is bubbling up through the yard drain, which is a soak-away into the beck, and has started to come through the fire door into the cellar. There is usually some water in the cellar, which is daily pumped through an outlet pipe straight into the beck. Go to Cottingham Boards and ask them to deliver a ton bag of sand, drop this off to block fire door. Alan Hellstrom (he has his plumber's office next door) and I clear drains by hand. This helps a bit.

3.00 p.m. The water in the yard is now flooding up to just below the sills of the cars. Have to use our van to get into the cars, to move them to higher ground. Leave work and six pumps in cellar working all O.K.

7.00 p.m. At home I get a call from Vicky, my daughter, to say she's on Hotham Road North and her car has stopped and is filling up with water on the inside. I set off to tow her in, but the water down Priory Road is too deep for a car, so return home and get the off-road Land Rover from my brother. We tow the car back, empty the water out and dry the car out at home. I then road-test the car and return to work to check on the flood. To my amazement Beck Bank is blocked off by the residents, because of the floods. Speak to Martin Haynes, leave car and walk to work. To my amazement the water is up to the third step by the office door, the yard is full, and the

***Next Day.** The flooded yard with the one ton bag of sand still blocking the fire door that leads down into the cellar. Creyke Beck runs right to left behind the far wall, topped with fencing. (Gavin Smith)*

cellar is flooded almost up to the ceiling. The beck water has got higher than the yard soak-away and the cellar outlet pipe, so it's flooded back in. In the cellar are our spare equipment, furniture and paper records for the Inland Revenue, plus the Cottingham St Mary's scouts' camping gear stored there by Martin Haynes for safe keeping — and it's all under water.

Tuesday 26th June

The yard is full of watery oil and the cellar still flooded. Ring the insurance company, Environmental Health, Yorkshire Water. Hire extra pumps from Champion Hire to pump water from the cellar, clear part of the yard so as to carry on working. Have to cancel some jobs, as limited parking available.

Postscript, February 2008

It took seven months to pump the cellar dry. It was once the basement of two circular gasholders, each about fifty foot wide and a good fourteen foot deep, which belonged to the Cottingham Gas Company (closed in 1902). Station Mills was built over them by Paley and Donkin, who still own the premises and rent part of it to Cottingham MOT Centre. Parts of the cellar floors normally have clear spring water bubbling up. After June 25th the cellar kept filling with water because the water table was so high. All the furniture and equipment (including the scout gear) was ruined but some of the paper records dried out O.K.

September 13, 2007. A view of the yard showing a large pump extracting water from the cellar into the yard, from where it could drain off through a soak-away into Creyke Beck. (Gavin Smith)

October 8, 2007. One corner of the cellar with flood-damaged goods still sitting in water. On June 25 the water was almost to the ceiling (out of shot), ruining the spare parts and equipment. (Gavin Smith)

Station Road

June 25. Cottingham station and the railway track were not flooded. They are on slightly raised ground with drainage ditches. (John Horsley)

A flooded station car park on June 25. Beyond the trees lie the grounds of the former Danish Bacon factory, Victoria's Way, and Mill Beck. (Mike Fee)

A view of the garages behind St Mary's Mount, the ground floor flats of which were badly flooded. The photo was taken from the wall above the railway station platform. (Mike Fee)

Victoria's Way

South end of Victoria's Way looking north in the evening of June 25. (Mike Fee)

The south side of the 'Square', Victoria's Way, looking west. (Hilary Nowell)

Victoria's Way looking north from the 'Square' towards the communal car park. (Hilary Nowell)

__June 26.__ Inside one of the houses in Victoria's Way this fridge-freezer had fallen over when it floated in the flood water. (Katrin McClure)

After the flood came the loss adjusters and the clearing out. Val Barker and neighbour Georgina Boughen prepare cardboard boxes donated by the Haltemprice Lions. (Terry Johnson)

The Mill Beck Flood

Peter McClure and Val Barker

Victoria's Way lies next to Mill Beck, just after it has been joined by Creyke Beck. The beck is first open and then culverted as it runs south-eastwards between the houses on its western bank and the grounds of the former Danish Bacon Factory and the Station car park on its eastern bank. It is briefly open again at the bottom of Victoria's Way and Station Road. The first sign of trouble was when one resident saw water from the beck flowing over into the road by about 8.30 in the morning. Then, at about ten o'clock Mrs Val Barker and Mr Terry Johnson noticed water coming into next door's back garden (no. 14) at the northern end of Victoria's Way, where the houses form a 'Square'. Half an hour later it was in their own garden (no. 16).

No. 16's back garden at about 11 a.m. (Val Barker)

The water was rising and the house was at risk. Mrs Barker rang the East Riding Council, Yorkshire Water and Flood Alert, but no help was forthcoming. Mr Johnson went round the corner to Cottingham Boards in Station Road to get some sandbags. When he got back with the second load he noticed that water from the beck had taken the line of least resistance between no. 10 and no. 12, and was entering the Square where, 'as usual, the drains did not work'.

Conservatory under a foot of water. (Val Barker)

The water rose incredibly quickly by 11.30 it was entering houses on the western side of the Square and some on the eastern side were flooded a short while later, by about 12.15. Another half an hour later it was inside no. 16 in the north-east corner of the Square. Mrs Barker and Mr Johnson rescued as much as they could, taking things upstairs and piling up as much furniture as they could off the floors. The conservatory and the rest of the ground floor were flooded to a depth of about a foot. The water continued to rise and a little after 1.30 p.m. Mrs Barker, Mr Johnson and other residents were forced to evacuate their homes.

Later that evening it stopped raining and at about two o'clock in the early hours, according to one resident, the flood waters suddenly dropped, as if someone had pulled out a plug.

Sitting room, with furniture piled up off the flooded floor. (Val Barker)

'The Square' in Victoria's Way, just after 1.30 p.m. when the residents had to evacuate their homes. (Hilary Nowell)

A week or so after the flood, sandbags and a pile of carpet underlay outside Val Barker's house. (Val Barker)

After the flood, ground floor rooms were chopped out and dried with the help of fans and dehumidifiers. (Val Barker)

Next day the East Riding Council delivered some sandbags in a lorry, in case further flooding occurred. To everyone's astonishment and dismay, the three young men who came in the lorry refused to help. They stood by and watched (mostly elderly) residents heave the bags off the lorry and carry them with immense effort to their own and others' houses. Some of the older men suffered injuries and health problems as a result. Mrs Barker said that she and other residents were sickened by this.

Then the loss adjusters came and the skips. Virtually everybody in the Square moved out, mostly away, but two couples stayed in caravans on the car park. One elderly lady was determined not to move out of her house. She lived upstairs, all through the clearing-out operation and the months of refurbishment, cheerfully supplying cups of tea to the workmen. Mrs Barker was treated well by her insurers and builders, and the refurbishment was done quickly and without hassle.

The one positive thing that came out of this terrible event was the way neighbours supported each other. The Square had always been a friendly enough place in the polite British way, but the warm community spirit that developed out of the floods was something quite different. One of the residents was generously given £100 by New Life Church, Hull, and he decided to share it with his neighbours. He organised a barbecue and invited everyone along. Some people brought bottles of wine and they all sat in the car park, decorated with balloons and coloured lights, and cheered themselves up. That new community spirit is still there, many months on.

Many of the Victoria's Way residents were back in their refurbished houses by January 2008, when flooding once again became a serious threat. On January 17 the beck filled to within an inch or two of the top of the bank. Sticks and hoes were used to try unblock the culvert exit next to the old Danish Bacon site. Someone phoned the East Riding Council for help, but the Council said that it was not responsible for the beck. So the residents and their friends did it themselves, at some personal risk and against the advice of the police, who came and watched for a while. Some residents bought some long-handled rakes and dragged out enormous quantities of rubbish, both from the beck and also from the screen where the beck becomes culverted for a second time, near the junction of Victoria's Way and Station Road. Branches and masses of wet leaves had turned the screen into a dam. They also pulled out a log that had jammed one of the two pipes at the end of the other culvert further upstream by the old Danish Bacon site. Once the beck and the screen had been cleared, the water level dropped by about four feet, it was reckoned. Even so, residents took it in turns to watch the beck water level right through the following night. The rubbish was later taken away by the Council.

The floods of June 25 have left their mark in more ways than one. Every time it rains hard, the residents of Victoria's Way feel anxiety welling up again. It was a close-run thing on January 17. Only prompt action by themselves and their friends prevented another flooding, and there have been more scares since.

The residents' barbecue in Victoria's Way later that summer, expressing their shared defiance and the deeper friendship that grew out of the flooding. (Val Barker)

One of the two caravans in the car park, where two Victoria's Way couples lived for several months after the flood. (Val Barker)

January 17, 2008. *Some of the debris dragged out of the beck. (Val Barker)*

January 17, 2008. *Residents using long-handled rakes to clear the Mill Beck screen, when the beck nearly flooded again. (Val Barker)*

PART TWO

PERSONAL EXPERIENCES

4. North Cottingham

North Cottingham (everywhere north of Harland Way and Northgate) experienced a great deal of water, but mercifully many fewer houses were flooded than in west and central Cottingham. The sequence begins with Park Lane and Grange Drive, then moves east to the King George V Playing Fields, Queen's Drive, Queen's Way, Mill Beck Lane, Northgate (east end) and Linden Avenue. For convenience, we have added the south side of Northgate at the level crossing gates and the northern end of Station Road.

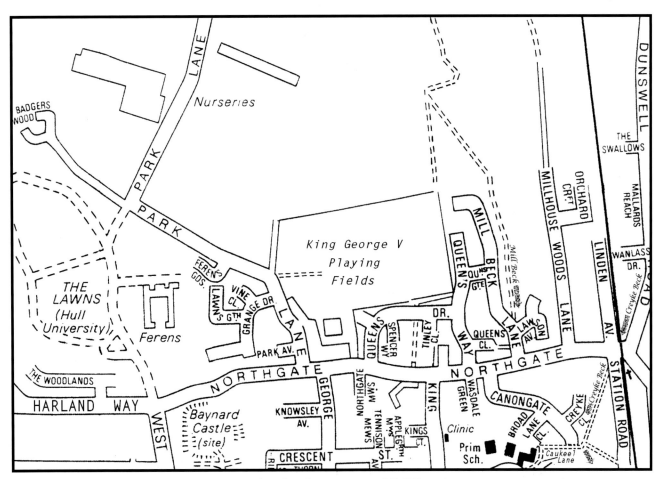

(Reproduced with permission of C J Utting.)

Park Lane

Flooded field on Park Lane looking towards greenhouses and the electricity sub-station. (John Horsley)

Water flooding both sides of Park Lane looking north-west, past the corner by the King George V Playing Fields. (John Horsley)

Park Lane looking south-east towards the junction with Grange Drive. (John Horsley)

Park Lane looking south at the junction with Grange Drive on the right. (John Horsley)

View down Grange Drive from Park Lane.
(John Horsley)

Park Lane looking north, with Grange Drive (left) and the
King George V Playing Fields (right, behind the trees).
(John Horsley)

Grange Drive

A view of Grange Drive through a rain-splashed window.
Note the waves created by the car at the junction with
Vine Close (opposite). (Geoff Bell)

Grange Drive, with water flooding across the grass verge
and footpath into people's gardens. Luckily the houses
stayed dry. (Geoff Bell)

King George V Playing Fields

The footpath from Park Lane into the King George V Playing Fields. (John Horsley) ...

... View from the end of the footpath looking east across the playing fields. (John Horsley) ...

... The King George V Playing Fields looking more like a river flood plain. (John Horsley) ...

... The southern edge of the playing fields showing water flowing into the back gardens of the houses in Queen's Drive, behind the hedges on the right. (John Horsley) ...

... King George V Playing Fields looking west towards the pavilion. Note the water flowing from the dyke (centre-left) into the field. (Martin Levitt)

King George V Playing Fields

Charles Levitt writes:

The pictures show the situation on the afternoon of the flood a few hours after the rain ceased. All were taken from the same point, where a footpath from Queen's Drive enters the park. Flooding was most severe on the south side of the park, where the land levels are lowest. Occasionally short-lived puddles of standing water occur in this area after 'normal' rainfalls, suggesting that the park has inadequate drainage. Surface drainage along the southern edge of the park is served by a substantial dyke about 6ft deep and almost as wide, which flows west to east. As well as park water, the dyke has a culverted input from a source west of the park. That input is so great that you can see in Picture 1 a flow of water from the ditch into the already flooded park.

1. King George V Playing Fields looking west towards the pavilion. Note the water over-flowing from the dyke (left, out of shot) into the field. (Martin Levitt)

2. King George V Playing Fields looking east, showing flood water that could not enter the culverted section of the dyke (right of picture). (Martin Levitt)

At about the point where the pictures were taken, the dyke itself goes into a culvert extending to the eastern edge of the park.

This culvert has a capacity far less than that of the dyke, which is why the dyke overflowed, as shown in Picture 2.

The culvert cannot receive any flood water from the northern and eastern sides of the park, hence the much more severe flooding in those areas, where the water was about 18in deep and covered about a quarter of the park area (Pictures 3 & 4).

3. King George V Playing Fields looking north from the back garden of no 10 Queen's Drive. (Martin Levitt)

4. King George V Playing Fields looking north . (Martin Levitt)

Queen's Drive

The eastern end of Queen's Drive backs onto the dyke on King George V Playing Fields.

Queen's Drive looking west. The water is flowing into the road from the King George V Playing Fields. (Martin Levitt)

Queen's Way

Paul Gibson writes:

The photographs show the extent of the flooding in Queen's Way caused by the breach in the drain on the south side of King George V playing fields. The flood water flowed down a neighbour's drive opposite to my house in the cul-de-sac which, after a period, surcharged the road drain and sewer, resulting in the 'river' you see in Picture 1.

Once the water in the road reached the level shown then the drainage system in the drive backed up and water then was forced out of the manhole in the drive to the rear of the house (Picture 2). This also resulted in further flooding due to rain water from the fall pipes as it could not drain away.

1. Water overflowing from the road drain and sewer, resulting in the 'river' along Queen's Way. (Paul Gibson)

2. Water forced out of the manhole in the drive.
(Paul Gibson)

There was about four inches of water under the floorboards and some neighbours lost electrical circuits due to shorting.

The rain eased about tea time, thankfully, otherwise the water may have topped the drives, which would then have had serious consequences. Fortunately the slightly contaminated water from the manhole ran to the end of the garden (Picture 3).

3. Water from the manhole ran to the end of the garden.
(Paul Gibson)

Amazingly all the floodwater had disappeared when we got up the following morning.

Mill Beck Lane

Mill Beck overtopping its banks, an unusual event. (John Horsley)

Northgate (east)

Northgate looking west towards Mill Beck Lane (right) and Canongate (left). (John Horsley)

Water vortexing into the road gully outside no. 18 Northgate, near the junction with Mill Beck Lane, late afternoon on June 25.
(John Horsley)

Northgate (east), Linden Avenue junction

Northgate looking north to the junction with Linden Avenue at 8.10 p.m., showing water diverting north into Linden Avenue and south towards Crossing Cottage (behind the photographer). (Fiona Nicholson)

Northgate at the junction with Linden Avenue, early evening. The raised bank of the railway crossing is turning water down into Linden Avenue, where it meets more water flooding from the ditch on the east side.
(Fiona Nicholson)

Looking south to houses on Northgate near the railway crossing. (Fiona Nicholson)

Northgate at the railway crossing, early evening, with no 1, Crossing Cottage, on the right. (Fiona Nicholson)

Creyke Beck flooding across the footpath which runs behind the commercial units at the north end of Station Road. The basement of Cottingham Cycle Centre, the other side of the wall, was flooded. (Fiona Nicholson)

Letter to America

Dave Fairburn

These are extracts from an e-mail that Dave Fairburn wrote over several days and sent to a friend in America. They begin on Tuesday 26 June, the day after the flooding, and end two days later.

Some days you remember all of your life. Yesterday was one of those days. It started out pretty much as any other, rain has been falling steadily throughout Sunday night, heavy but not exceptional. I was in two minds whether or not to phone the quarry before setting off for work, to see if the orders had been put on hold until the weather improved. I decided to go. When I got to my yard to pick my truck up, the rain was getting heavier, sod it, I should have phoned in. I drove to the quarry regretting not making that phone call. It was 6 a.m. when I arrived. I asked Graham, the weighbridge clerk, if everything had gone on hold. 'Not yet, but it's still early. I can't see much happening today. You should get a load of stone for the St Stephen's Square development job but it's not due until 8 o'clock. Go wait down the quarry and I'll give you a shout later.'

The rain was now falling like stair rods. I couldn't imagine anyone wanting stone that day, let alone tarmac, but at 8 o'clock Graham called me to put a load of type 2 stone on. This was bad news. Type 2 for St Stephen's meant that it was being laid through a paving machine. Bad news in as much as it meant that I would be about an hour on site discharging my load and, coupled with the two hours waiting to load it, meant that I had turned out for peanuts.

When I got to the weighbridge to tare off and get my delivery note, Graham was on the phone. He hung up. 'That was Nuttall's (customer at St Stephens), they have just put it on hold.' 'Shall I tip it back onto the stockpile and go home?' I asked hopefully. 'No take it. I've already made the ticket out.' When I arrived on site I saw the lads waiting in their crew bus. One shouted a lot of what may have been French at me but on reflection was more probably Anglo-Saxon. He held his hand out of the window

A back garden under water in Linden Avenue, 7.10 p.m. (Fiona Nicholson)

and snatched the ticket from me and it disappeared inside the crew bus, only to appear moments later, signed. I hesitated before asking him where he wanted me to put the load but I deciphered from the reply that I could tip it anywhere I wanted and then go. I didn't hang about long enough for him to change his mind.

I arrived home at 10.30 a.m. and started to continue my letter to you. I typed the date in and then decided to make a cup of coffee to have with my uneaten snap whilst I could think of something else to write that would bore the socks off you. Looking out on to my garden I could see standing water on the path. I was just thinking that I had never seen that before when the phone rang. It was my uncle telling me that his garden was flooding. He has been having this trouble since he bought the house a month back. Basically whoever laid the patio and path put the drainage gully at the high point. It's funny to see, the gully is stuck up like an island when it rains. It doesn't start to flow down the gully until the standing water is two inches deep. I said I would pop round to see if I could dip it for levels so that we would know where to put drainage channels in and which way the falls should run.

On the way round there the local radio station was giving out weather warnings. I looked at his patio again but couldn't do anything to remedy the situation at that moment, had a cup of tea with him and came home, after first picking up some meat in the village for tea. The standing water was now about calf level and my boots were in the garage. I put the meat on and started making pastry for a meat pie. The precipitation was not slight. The next time I looked out the waters had risen a further three inches and were now lapping onto the patio. I was starting to get concerned. My neighbour was out in his garden. 'Have you ever seen it like this before? Do you think that we'll be all right?' 'Yeah, Cottingham has never flooded.' I'm not sure who I was trying to convince.

I turned the radio on. The reports were

The south end of Linden Avenue, looking north, at 7.30 p.m. The road was inundated at first from Northgate but later from the overflowing ditch between the trees and the railway line (right). Some residents also noticed spring water welling up under their homes.
(Fiona Nicholson)

getting more dire by the minute. Hull and the East Riding was becoming impassable, major roads were being closed. I carried on making my meat pie just in case the power went off later. A Council official came on the radio, they were running out of sandbags and what few were left were being delivered by the army to the areas of greatest need. I looked out of the back bedroom window, water, water everywhere.

Nita came home from work, and Nita being Nita wasn't flustered, wasn't panicky and wasn't hysterical. She said that she had some sandbags at the bottom of the garden and, blow me, she had. She started to sandbag the airbricks. That girl never ceases to amaze me, barrowing sandbags through a foot of water whilst drinking tea. I said that I thought it was a waste of time as the underfloor area was already starting to flood and the water was not yet up to the airbricks. As she pointed out it was all we could do and it may slow the ingression down.

I lifted the trap door under the stairs so that I could monitor the water rising under the floor, and carried on cooking dinner so that Davy could have a hot meal when he came home. If we were to be flooded out then by jingo we would do it on a full stomach. Nita carried on sandbagging the house. It was still raining heavily. Debris and detritus was flowing out of the garden past the back door and out into the street, leaves, twigs, June-drop apples, a fishing smack. I looked under the floor before we all sat down for tea, I looked under the floor after we had all eaten. The water had risen three inches. I looked out of the back door. Debris and detritus was flowing out of the street past the back door and into the garden, leaves, twigs, June drop apples, a VLCC. The dyke

The north end of Linden Avenue on the evening of June 25.
(Dave Fairburn)

No. 48 Linden Avenue. (Dave Fairburn)

opposite our house had burst its banks, the street was now awash.

Hmm, things had looked better. We took the decision to move all the furniture upstairs except for the dog's basket. They worked like Trojans, I was proud of them both — the dog had her own views. By now the water level had reached the top of the stretcher wall, only the thickness of the floor joists separated the water from downstairs floor. I looked outside. United Towing had managed to get a towline on the VLCC, the fishing smack had cast a seine net, and it had stopped raining. What little we could do had now been done.

I checked under the floor and the water had risen another inch. We still had two inches of freeboard to play with before it came through the house. Outside the neighbours were congregating in the Avenue, liquor was in evidence, kids were playing with the dogs, people were laughing and chatting. One neighbour commented that it was approaching Biblical proportions. Dear God, we still have the famine and the pestilence to come. They had all done what they could. With a bit more warning we could have organised a street party with a Venetian theme. In the words of the Italians, *que sera sera*, or was it the French? No, it was Doris Day, grand lass, one of my dad's favourites, he remembered her singing with the Ambrose Orchestra before she became a virgin. Came back in at about 10 p.m., looked under the floor, two inches of freeboard, we may yet get away with it. Took pity on the dog and moved her to higher ground. Nothing else we could do, we weren't in mortal danger, went to bed and slept like a log.

Awoke the following morning at 7 a.m. I'd had a lie in, dog greeted me and the carpets didn't squelch under my feet. Peered under the floorboards, ten inches of freeboard. After a cuppa I went out with the dog for a paddle round the village. Wow, had we been lucky, the extent of the flooding was amazing.

It is now Thursday, three days after the rains, a lot of major roads in Hull are still shut off. My veg plot round the corner down Dunswell Lane is still under two feet of water, the crops will probably be knackered for this year. Yesterday my sticklebacks and tadpoles could be seen swimming across my lawn, so they are done for, but Hey, we haven't suffered at all. Others have paid with their lives, five so far, and many, many homes have been wrecked.

Linden Avenue looking south towards Northgate. The trees mark the line of the old field dyke, which drains into Creyke Beck via two pipes under the railway embankment close to Northgate crossing. On June 25 the beck water was higher than the pipes, so the dyke overflowed. (Dave Fairburn)

PART TWO

PERSONAL EXPERIENCES

5. East Cottingham

East Cottingham (everywhere east of the railway line) suffered a lot of flooding along Dunswell Road and roads off it (North Moor Lane and Wanlass Drive), mainly because of Creyke Beck overflowing. There was a little flooding along New Village Road and roads off it but we have photographic evidence from June 25 only for Devon Street and for the south end of New Village Road. Some houses on Endyke Lane were flooded by water from Thwaite Lake but we have no photographs of this area on June 25 apart from Stephenson's Walk. At the south end Croxby Primary School (off Bricknell Avenue) was severely inundated and the building was out of use for some time.

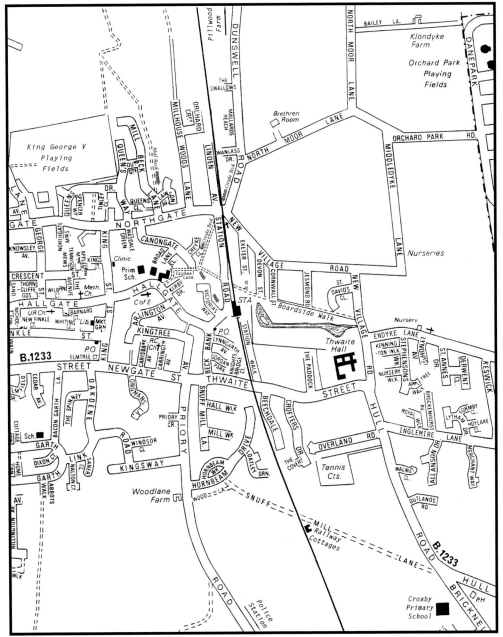

(Reproduced with permission of C J Utting.)

Dunswell Lane, A1079 Underpass

On June 25 and 26 torrents of water poured off the fields into the underpass on Dunswell Lane.

June 26. Still frames taken from a video show water pouring off the fields and down into the underpass (looking east).
(Gwen Mathers)

A day later .....

Surface water and spring water were still draining off the fields ...(Imogen Mathers)

... but the water level in the underpass was starting to drop.
(Imogen Mathers)

Dunswell Road (North), Pillwood Farm

June 25. Creyke Beck flowing across Dunswell Road by Pillwood Farm. (Jean Durnford)

Next Day, 10 a.m. *A similar view of Pillwood Farm showing even more flooding from the fields to the west. (Fiona Nicholson)*

June 25. The inundated front garden of the Durnford's house and nursery on Dunswell Road, opposite Pillwood Farm. (Jean Durnford)

Next day, morning. *Entrance to Pillwood Farm from Dunswell Road. (Fiona Nicholson)*

June 26, morning. A view of the flooded fields at Pillwood Farm looking west. (Fiona Nicholson)

June 26, 10.45 a.m. The flooded farmyard at Pillwood Farm. (Fiona Nicholson)

June 26. Flooded buildings at Pillwood Farm. (Fiona Nicholson)

June 26, evening. Looking east from Pillwood Farm. (Fiona Nicholson)

Dunswell Road (south)

Dunswell Road looking south to Northgate, near the junction with North Moor Lane (left). Creyke Beck is beyond the railing (right). (John Horsley)

Gardens behind the Dunswell Road houses (west side) became ponds. (John Goodby)

Wanlass Drive

Wanlass Drive under water from Creyke Beck, viewed from Dunswell Road on the evening of June 25. The culvert under Wanlass Drive is quite low, forcing a great deal of beck water over the top and down the drive. (John Goodby)

We Just Lost Everything

Bim and Sandra Pougher

On June 25th 2007 Wanlass Drive was flooded by Creyke Beck and by water from a lake behind houses in Dunswell Road. Printed here are edited extracts from a recorded interview with Sandra and Albert (known to his friends as 'Bim') Pougher, who were still living in a caravan in their drive on February 5, 2008, when Peter McClure (transcript editor) and Tony Grundy (recording engineer) visited them. The transcription was made by Christine Gould-Knappett. Most of the photographs are by Dean Roberts, husband of Bim and Sandra's elder daughter Vicky. The first question was 'When did it start raining?'

SANDRA: On the Sunday, it started on the Sunday heavy, didn't it? It was raining all day Sunday, and it was on the Monday we flooded. That was when my [younger] daughter rang at lunchtime to say that she had it coming in her conservatory at Kingswood. So I said 'Don't worry, Ellie, it won't be too bad, I'll get to you when I've finished my ironing'. I rang Bim at work and told him, and I was just stood ironing at maybe about half past one? And I just looked round and our back lawn was like a paddling pool. I rang him at work again and I said 'Ooh, I don't know about Ellie, ours is like a paddling pool'.

The far end of Wanlass Drive viewed from the end of the Pougher's drive. The water is moving up the drive from Creyke Beck. (Dean Roberts)

The Pougher's driveway under water. (Dean Roberts)

Then I got a phone call from Ellie. 'Mum, don't try to get through, the Fire Brigade's here, they're getting us to safety, all the roads is blocked, you can't get through.' I said it was on the patio, and I rang Bim at work. I said 'It's now on the patio', and Bim said 'Don't worry, it won't come in, because we're a little bit higher'. And by the time that he got home, within half an hour, it was up the drive at the

Looking south from in front of the house and along the drive. (Dean Roberts)

front way, but it was coming very fast at the back, and it was in the back conservatory. It was from the lake at the back of those big houses, and so it gushed there in very fast. And it was coming up there from the Beck up the front. I would say that by half past two that afternoon, it was up to our knees — we had

Bim Pougher stands at his back garden door looking down into a pond of half-submerged plants and garden furniture. (Dean Roberts)

The Pougher's back garden. It started to flood from the lake beyond the fence, but there was even more force of water from Creyke Beck down Wanlass Drive, as the ripples show. (Dean Roberts)

no shoes on — and that was how fast it was! That's how quick it happened!

The rain was very heavy, very heavy, it was that heavy, torrential. Dunswell Road — it broke the drains and was just gushing up into the air. It was horrendous. They'd stopped the traffic going through but you'd still got people with the 4 x 4s forcing their way through …

BIM: Causing waves, flooding water into people's homes.

The Pougher's front garden, with a half-drowned statue. (Dean Roberts)

SANDRA: So there was nine of us, two dogs and two cats, all in Dean's bungalow in Canongate. Because my daughter [Ellie], they'd got her out to safety, with the baby and their dog, then there was us with our dog, two cats and us, and we'd nowhere to go, all of us. So we went there, and at about half past ten that night, Dean said 'I think it's stopped raining!' We stayed there overnight, and then we walked round next morning, and it wasn't raining then, but it was in one heck of a mess really. Everywhere was just … well we just lost everything, didn't we?

BIM: We got three family heirlooms out, didn't we? And we got them to somebody, we managed to get them taken, 'cause them three items is each individually insured, on separate policies.

SANDRA: On the Thursday, Rainbow came. Bim had gone to Driffield and it was me here. And they were drying-out people, that bring the dehumidifiers and everything, and they came from Scotland. And they just came in the bungalow, there was two of them, and they just said 'Right, I'm sorry but everything's going out'. And they just got every mortal thing and it was like two bonfires on the drive. And me and Dean helped 'em with the carpets, that was it. Everything. Everything was there — our beds, everything, cooker — every mortal thing. And that was it, really. And there was things that we can't replace — boxes of photos that was in the bottom of the wardrobes was soaked. Nothing will be the same.

1. August 2007. *The Pougher's kitchen.*
(Dean Roberts)

2. September 2007. *The Pougher's bedroom.*
(Dean Roberts)

Bim and Sandra showed some of Dean's photographs.

That's the kitchen (*Picture 1*). They took everything out. You can see there, they've ripped it all out. That was the bedroom (*Picture 2*). The water's gone down but this was wet, and all in the cupboards was wet, so all these were rove out. This was this back room (*Picture 3*) where they've took all the carpet up, and just rived it all out. That was the hallway (*Picture 4*), where all the units were and the bedroom furniture. They got them into the hallway and then out of the front door. 'Cause we'd left things in drawers, you see, and they was taking them out. They took the carpets out, took the units out, took the bed, the bedding and everything — they just took it all out. We were planning to go on holiday. They came on Saturday afternoon, the first loss adjusters, and we went on holiday on the Sunday.

3. September 2007. *The Pougher's back room.*
(Dean Roberts)

4. September 2007. *The Pougher's hallway.*
(Dean Roberts)

BIM: That's right, they give us fifteen hundred pounds to buy clothes, so we got some clothes, and our cases had gone, they was in the wardrobe, they'd gone. When we say they give us fifteen hundred pounds, it was there when we come back — there was a cheque. We was away for ten days.

SANDRA: A lot of stuff went out on the Thursday before — and the loss adjusters just came, they put a lot of furniture in the garage, but some things come on the front drive. And the loss adjuster just came, with all his board and everything, and just looked at everything, in the garage and on the drive. Did it that way — there was nothing in the house — he just opened the wardrobes and said that all these has got to come out. They didn't complete the job on the Thursday, but when we came back, then

5. September 2007. *The Pougher's kitchen with broken pipes. (Dean Roberts)*

6. August 2007. *The Pougher's lounge, with their pride and joy, the Cumberland stone fireplace still there. It cracked when the floor joists were cut, so they have since replaced it with a plain wall. (Dean Roberts)*

they came and a lot got taken away. The carpets was left on the drive for about four weeks — it was a different loss adjuster that came for carpets, so we was waiting quite a few weeks, and then he came, and then he said 'Right, they can now go to the Council'.

BIM [*pointing to a photograph, Picture 5*]: That is after a team of Polish lads had moved in from S*****'s [the firm of builders supplied by the insurance company]. They employed all these Polish lads. There were four and they couldn't speak English. We had to have a plumber all the time on standby because they was breaking the pipes, so there was as much water again, it did a lot of damage again. We just couldn't believe what we were looking at. And this is the lounge (*Picture 6*). The best part of that was this, the fireplace, Cumberland stone all the way through. Now that is gone.

SANDRA: It's cracked. They said they could clean it out, patch it up with what we can get as near as possible to a match, but it was a special colour, so we said 'It's got to go'. And it was from floor to ceiling, as you'll see, all with a mahogany finish on. And it's all gone, gone, just a plain wall with nothing.

BIM: That is the small toilet (*Picture 7*) and I'm pointing up to the roof, where they've ploughed a sledgehammer through — hitting the tiles off with hammers and with crow-bars, just knocking and banging. And I just went in and I said 'What are you doing?' And the ceiling came in.

*At this point Sandra left the caravan to talk to the builder, whose men had put the electric sockets in the wrong places, behind where the kitchen units were to go. Bim went on to describe how the builders had done needless damage by doing a full strip of the kitchen walls, instead of a half strip. Because of the flooding it was necessary to take out the old under-floor heating ducts. When Bim said to the builder 'Are you going to take these out, S*****'s?' he was told:*

'We'll have to have a team of specialists in for that'. So I said to him, I said 'How do you work that out?' 'Well', he said, 'that is one hell of a job'. And I said to him 'Why, the best thing you could do, I said, is to leave that as now, and I will get another advice on that. Then I spoke to Don Hardwick, and I showed him the set-up, and he said to me, 'Mr. Pougher,' he said, 'if you're

7. September 2007. *Bim pointing to where the plumbers ploughed a sledgehammer through the roof of the small toilet. (Dean Roberts)*

August 2007. Bim standing on an under-floor heating duct in the lounge before he and Don Hardwick stripped it out. (Dean Roberts)

August 2007. Caravan and skip parked in front of the Pougher's home. (Dean Roberts)

willing to help me to strip 'em,' he said, 'we'll have things out within half a day'. And that is what we did, and we paid Don Hardwick to strip them out and, of course, a team [from the builders] — six of 'em — turned up on the Monday to take the air ducts out — gone!! [Stephen Edmond's haulage came and] put 'em in the van and took them to the tip. You know, I think where they've gone wrong along the line is they've called the outsides tradesmen in from Leeds, Bradford — 'cause that's all that's visited this property is from out of town, and I think they've just left our local lads out of it completely, thinking they could get it done cheaper — and it hasn't worked out that way at all.

The insurance company offered hotel accommodation while the house was being put right, but Bim and Sandra preferred to live in a caravan on the drive. The insurance company gave them £5,000, to which the Poughers added some of their own money to get one that was livable in. When the transporter arrived, the caravan was left on the road, for the Poughers to work out how to move it into their driveway:

So we had to set to then, getting it sited, getting so much put in, getting electric connected up properly, and that took what, four days, five days? 'Cause you know, once again, Don Hardwick's a good friend of mine and he brought his tractor in, and he helped us that way to get it sited. The pets went in the kennels. We run a bill up to eight hundred and forty pound. We got a phone call from the kennels to say that the oldest cat died through, we knew, through stress, because we did salvage that cat out of the water. You see, as from there, everything went, went downhill.

About three weeks after the flooding, Bim was in a traffic accident on his way back from Driffield, where he sells fish at the market. His truck was a write-off.

It was a bad shunt, it was bad rain, once again, heavy rain. I don't know if you remember the rain, fortnight three weeks after. It was really really heavy heavy rain, everything was a washout. There was a van parked parked on Woodmansey. He was delivering to this particular house. The air-vent van in front of me, he thought he was going to pull out, so he braked, and of course I went for my brakes — wet! Spanked him, wrote the van off. And as from there, you know, the month just progressed poor, you know. We just had bad luck all the way. It was as though someone had ... had measles and poking me, you know, thinking 'Go on, what can go wrong now, what can go wrong now?'

Sandra's health suffered, the caravan was burgled and it was hard keeping their spirits up.

We're both in our sixties, and obviously like thousands more it's something we could've done without. My heart goes out to everybody who has been flooded, and anyone who hasn't been flooded, they can't explain it, because when we used to see it on the television before, we used to think 'Gad, them poor people', especially in York, 'cause it just seemed to be week after week after week in York, you know.

What would we do if it happened to us? You know, we spoke with the best will in the world, we're in a cul de sac, we're tucked out the way, it just won't happen. And it's just turned our lives, oh, we've gone backwards, we've gone backwards, there's no two ways about it. In this past eight months, we've carried on working because for the simple reason we're self employed, and we're not that kind of people to throw the hat in. We keep going no matter what it throws at us.

And at the moment this is where we're living — in the caravan. Seven months down the line it isn't good, like thousands more — we're not by ourselves. When you go out the small bedroom to the rear of the caravan, once it gets locked up on a night time, we've got the central heating on, it's quite cosy! The caravans are O.K. for holiday, for

August 2007. Sandra and Bim with their surviving cat in the caravan. The caravan is cosy, up to a point, but as Bim says 'Caravans are O.K. for a holiday but to live in them permanent, I wouldn't, you know.' (Dean Roberts)

a fortnight out at the seaside, but to live in them permanent, I wouldn't, you know. These people who live in a static caravan permanent, they've got to be a special breed. I come out that bedroom half past five in a morning into here. I come from maybe sixty-six, sixty-eight degrees into forty-six, and you try to get shaved. Fair enough, we've got hot water on tap all the time, but once or twice these cold frosty mornings, we've been frozen pipes, and we've made sure that we've got enough water to get a wash, and a shave, to go to work the following morning, even to make a cup of tea. But, you know, it isn't good. My wife does her very very best trying to cook a meal and, you know, she does well.

We try to make it easy as time goes on, but when we try to make phone calls to the contractors, to the insurance, to the loss adjusters, 'Yes Mr. Pougher, we've got your message, we'll ring you back within the hour'. Maybe a week later, ten days later: 'Oh, we're just returning your phone call, Mr Pougher. We understand, looking at our computer, the e-mails what's been sent, we understand you're having problems....' We're having bloody big problems, I can tell you! You know, there's no-one is listening to us. It'll never be the same — something like it was, what's liveable, and we can say 'Well, yeah, fair enough, we've had a rough do', but now we're going to leave that behind us, and try and get back to some normality.

Bim and Sandra moved back into their house on April 5th. In the meantime the builders had gone out of business, so the Poughers arranged for the remaining work to be done by local contractors.

June 2008. *Look, no caravan! (Peter McClure)*

Dunswell Road (south), North Moor Lane Junction

June 25, about 5 p.m. Creyke Beck opposite North Moor Lane (right, out of shot), with Wanlass Drive junction to the left. The water in the beck is level with the pavement. (John Goodby)

Looking east along North Moor Lane (south) from the junction with Dunswell Road. North Moor Lane is lower than Dunswell Road and a few houses were flooded at this end of the lane. (John Horsley)

Dunswell Road (south)

June 25, about 5 p.m. *A house alongside the Creyke Beck on Dunswell Road. (John Horsley)*

Creyke Beck later in the evening (7.40 p.m.) not far from the junction with Northgate and the 'Ducks Crossing' road-sign. (Fiona Nicholson)

June 25, 7.15 p.m. *Water spilling from Creyke Beck across Dunswell Road. Diversion sign still lying by the roadside from earlier roadworks. (Fiona Nicholson)*

Creyke Beck at the Northgate level crossing, late afternoon. Notice the reverse flow of the water backing up from the culvert beneath the railway crossing. (John Horsley)

Boardside Walk and Devon Street

The Boardside Walk runs along the northern boundary of Thwaite gardens and leads from the railway station to New Village Road. The section in the dip by the station was only passable wearing wellingtons, or getting wet feet, for several days after June 25.

June 25. Flooded rear gardens in Devon Street.
(Rachel Waters)

June 27, 6.45 p.m. Boardside Walk, looking towards the station, at the junction with Exeter Street, still under water.
(Rachel Waters)

June 26, 4.30 p.m. View, looking east, from the snicket at the end of St. David's Close. The New Village Road end of Boardside Walk is submerged. (Pat Elliott)

June 26, afternoon. The New Village Road end of Boardside Walk still flowing with water from Thwaite Lake. (Katrin McClure)

Middledyke Lane

June 26, early morning. Landscape gardener's lorry creating a water feature in Middledyke Lane. (Peter Kerr)

Endyke Lane

Endyke Lane

June 26, about 4 p.m. One of several properties on the north side of Endyke Lane. This photograph shows water still lying in the front drive and on the pavement, and the water mark at the base of the fence. (Pat Elliott)

June 26. The fields to the north of Endyke Lane were still under water. (Pat Elliott)

New Village Road (south)

Cottingham Bowling Club is situated at the southern end of New Village Road near the junction with Hull Road and Thwaite Street.

June 25. The all-weather bowling green. (Denys Abba)

A view of another flooded bowling green. (Denys Abba)

Stephenson's Walk

Stephenson's Walk from a motorist's perspective on June 25. (Denys Abba)

The floodwaters in Stephenson's Walk. (Denys Abba)

A rare chance for some boating, late afternoon in Stephenson's Walk. (Denys Abba)

The Snuff Mill Gates Island

Fr John Leeman

Snuff Mill Lane follows the route of the former Cottingham Beck, running beside the wide naturalised verge (where the beck has been replaced by a sewer), south-east of the Mill House between Hornbeam Drive and Bricknell Avenue/Hull Road. It is crossed by the Hull-Beverley railway line, and at the south-east side of the crossing stand two former railway cottages, in one of which I reside. This is a very nice, unspoilt lane with mature hedges and trees and an abundance of flowers and wildlife, adjoining some open fields. We welcome people to enjoy the lane, which is used a lot for cycling, and often by children, walking parties, mothers with prams and young kiddies, and happy dogs banished from many parks; here they are all free from the dangers of traffic. Although near to urban development, the area has an atmosphere of being totally 'in the country'.

It had been raining continuously, and on the Monday there were lakes of standing water on areas of the fields both west (to Priory Road) and east (to Bricknell Avenue) around the railway, where there are always springs and ponds, with also some water coming down from the Cottingham area. Serious flooding resulted in severe damage to the (Croxby) school on the Bricknell Avenue junction, which was closed for many months afterwards.

26 June. The playground of Croxby Primary School under water. Opened in 1964, the school was built on marshland between Snuff Mill Lane and Bricknell Avenue opposite a field on Hull Road known as 'Crooked Stile Horn' which seems to have been corrupted to 'Croxby'. (Katrin McClure)

There was also a lot of water in our two gardens, one of which already has a sizeable ornamental pond. Although the hedgerow and grassed beck-route were waterlogged, the lane was passable, but had very large pools and puddles where the surface is badly rutted and pot-holed, making travelling difficult for pedestrians, cycles, etc.

The two cottages and pedestrian gated crossing, however, although more or less surrounded by water, were luckily on slightly raised ground, and remained secure. The immediate flooding did not seem to last long, but the damage that was inflicted to localised areas had repercussions which are still not resolved almost a year later.

Croxby Primary School

Croxby Primary School is at the northern end of Bricknell Avenue near the junction with Hull Road. Photos by Katrin McClure.

This is Croxby Primary School playground, sitting in a lake of water, the day after the flood. It was the only school in the village that was actually flooded and the damage was massive. The Bricknell Avenue area escaped relatively unscathed from the great rains of June 2007. But, as Head Teacher David Ledgard explained in an interview for the Hull Daily Mail (June 18, 2008), the deluge of June 15 had turned the school grounds into a 'huge sponge', so the ground was saturated when the next deluge arrived on June 25 and the water had nowhere to go.

Staff and pupils were horrified to see water pouring into the building. Mr Ledgard decided to close the school immediately. He told David Paine, the Hull Daily Mail reporter 'At one point we were on the phones talking to parents knee-deep in water.' A pupil, Daniel Hirst, is quoted as saying that 'It was quite scary and watching the water come in was horrible. It was really upsetting to see all the books get covered in water.' According to Mr Ledgard, half a million gallons of water had to be pumped out of the building, and the school lost much of its equipment and most of the children's projects.

Three weeks after the flood the abandoned school was being cleared into skips and dried out (note the dehumidifiers in the photo.) For the rest of the summer term the school's staff and 360 pupils travelled by bus to the University on Cottingham Road to have their lessons. In September the pupils returned to the school, where they were taught partly in the new wing of the main building and partly in mobile classrooms. It was not until April 2008 that the mobiles were finally dispensed with, following the refurbishment of the school.

PART TWO

PERSONAL EXPERIENCES

6. South Cottingham

South Cottingham (west of the railway line and south of Thwaite Street, Newgate Street and South Street) got off most lightly. There have been a few but scattered reports of flooded houses there and we have received photographs of June 25 only for Priory Road, Hornbeam Drive and Loatley Green.

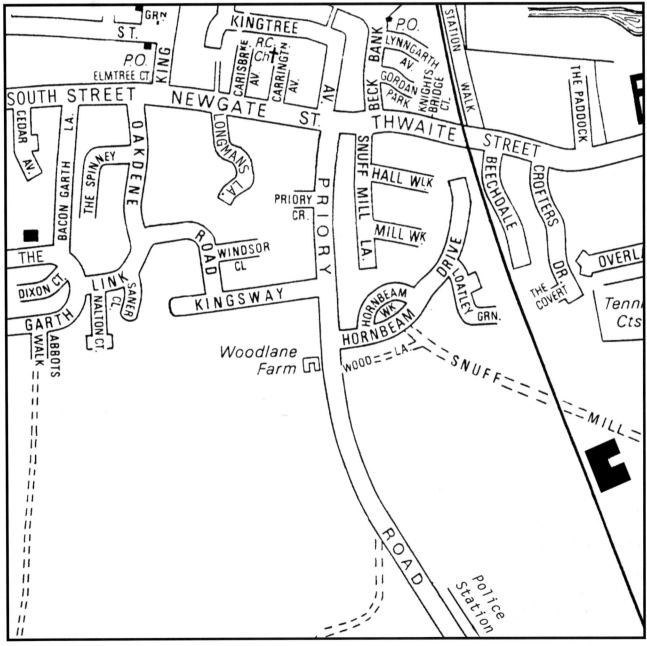

(Reproduced with permission of C J Utting.)

Priory Road

Within the boundaries of Cottingham, only the Humberside Police HQ, on the extreme southern edge, was seriously affected. Further south, over the Hull boundary, there was extensive flooding and the road was closed for several days.

Kingston upon Hull

Hull, June 26, mid-day. *Priory Road near Colwell Avenue. (John Frith)*

June 26. *An inundated back garden in Priory Road, Cottingham. (Katrin McClure)*

June 25, 1.42 p.m. *Priory Road looking south towards increasing amounts of surface water. In the half-distance on the left is the entrance to the Humberside Police HQ, which was eventually flooded. (John Frith)*

The Snuff Mill Tail-Race

Cyril Carter

I live on the northern side of Hornbeam Walk and the mill race (a narrow brick-walled channel from the former watermill) ran directly under my garden. When it was culverted, one brick wall was removed to make the width for the wide-bore pipe, but the other was left in. Recently I needed to remove a couple of trees growing beside the track of the former watercourse, and there were barrow-loads of bricks from the buried wall to be moved. The piped area was skimmed with concrete and covered with topsoil. In the gardens of both of my adjacent neighbours is an inspection cover, but the only evidence on my land is a noticeable dip where the in-fill has gradually sunk.

During the torrential rains this lower area flooded like a long pond to a depth of about nine inches following the route, and there was surface water over the gardens. I think that this was just trapped on the clay soil by the sheer volume of the downpour, and it ran across and between the bungalows and out on to the road. This was completely flooded, a few inches deep, with water half way up both pavements. Fortunately our buildings were slightly higher and there was no damage to them. The water was flowing generally towards the Snuff Mill Lane area and the railway, roughly along the route of the former Beck, and some properties on Hornbeam Drive were flooded.

In the morning there was nothing to be seen, and I cut the grass!

Aerial view of Snuff Mill. The grass strip to the right of the road above Snuff Mill house is the line of the culverted Mill Beck. Cyril Carter's house on Hornbeam Walk is at the bottom right, just out of shot. (Ken Green Collection)

Snuff Mill tail-race (that part of the mill race downstream from the mill wheel) is shown in this old postcard at the point where it rejoins the main Mill Beck channel (just appearing on the left) south of the site of the watermill. Cottingham Hall, demolished in 1935, is just visible in the distance to the right of the dilapidated footbridge. (Robert McMillan Collection)

Some Birthday!

Pat Elliott

Whilst I shall remember Monday 25 June 2007 as my husband's 58th birthday, many Cottingham residents will recollect it for their lives being turned upside down. We woke about 7.00 a.m. to the sound of it raining. At eight John left for Humberside Airport and encountered no problems reaching there. I, heeding the radio announcements 'not to travel unless your journey is absolutely necessary', decided to spend the day pottering about. As I washed the pots I noticed water collecting in the gutters and lower parts of the roads of Loatley Green and Hornbeam Drive, so that by about 9.20, when John rang to say that he had abandoned his business trip, I warned him of flooding down our lane.

Arriving home about 10.30, John related how he had been stuck in a queue of traffic on the Humber Bridge road (A164) after the Swanland roundabout, having been hit by a wall of water as it came off the fields, and had to return home via Kirk Ella, Willerby Road, Hotham Road and Priory Road as the traffic ahead seemed to be at a standstill. He was amazed to find my warning of our flooding to be true, assuming it had been an exaggeration, and said that Priory Road was beginning to flood.

By eleven o'clock our roads were becoming streams of continuous water flowing past the house from two directions, primarily from our right, that is further up Hornbeam Drive, and from our left, chiefly from Hornbeam Walk, uniting at our corner to flow down Loatley Green and presumably, somehow, beyond. A secondary arm was flowing down Hornbeam Drive itself. But where was this water coming from? Had Thwaite Street flooded and it was flowing down the snicket by the side of the railway line? Steadily the volume and depth of water increased. By lunchtime it was up to the middle of the wheels of cars as they ploughed through, some causing waves over the adjacent pavements and gardens, as they paid little heed to the situation.

Hornbeam Drive, flowing with water at about 3 p.m. as seen from no. 30. (Pat Ellliott)

Loatley Green from the corner with Hornbeam Drive at about 3 p.m. (Pat Elliott)

I rang my parents, who live in Wasdale Green, to check their situation and they, thankfully, were unaware that there was any problem. I resigned myself to sitting in our dining room, which overlooks the garden, watching the water level rise, first in the areas around the lawn, then the middle of the lawn, then the paving upwards towards the garage door, a depth of one and half bricks. At the front the 'river' rose over the kerb up to the edge of the lawn, penetrating any lower parts. You felt helpless, like Mickey Mouse in *The Sorcerer's Apprentice,* crying STOP but nothing was listening.

About three o'clock, sensing the severity of the situation, I photographed our immediate area, then waited. Between 4.30 and 5.00 came a sign that the waters were receding — a sliver of pavement was visible at the edge of the front lawn. With the realisation that the waters had peaked and the fear of flooding had passed, the sick feeling in the bottom of your stomach lessened. Nevertheless, the 'river' continued to surge relentlessly down our roads. It was still flowing at 7.30 in the evening when friends from Beechdale came to visit but were unable to reach us as they had not anticipated the situation which they beheld and were not adequately shod, indicating just how localised the flooding was. Gradually the rain eased and had stopped by bedtime about 10.30.

The story continues on page 150 in 'Out and About on Tuesday 26 June'.

August 2007. A caravan and skip in West End Road.
(Katrin McClure)

August 2007. A builder's portaloo and skip in West End Road.
(Katrin McClure)

August 2007. A skip in the driveway of Bim and Sandra
Poucher's house in Wanlass Drive. *(Dean Roberts)*

PART TWO

PERSONAL EXPERIENCES

7. Cottingham After the Flood

The devastation wrought by the floods gradually became more visible, as ruined carpets and furniture appeared on house drives. Then in the drives or on the verges came skips, large caravans and eventually builders' vans, while 'SITE SAFETY' notices appeared in the front windows of homes. The sequences of photographs and stories conclude with a detailed account of two walks around Cottingham the day after the flood. Taking in parts of south, central, north and east Cottingham, it also fills in some of the photographic gaps of June 25.

August 2007. Site safety notices in the window of a house in Eppleworth Road and a pile of flood-damaged furniture in the garden. (Katrin McClure)

March 2008. An evacuated flat in George Street. (Dorothy Catterick)

August 2007. Two house frontages on the north side of Eppleworth Road, a pile of damaged timber in one drive and a large caravan in the other. (Katrin McClure)

Out and About on Tuesday 26 June

Pat Elliott

Amazingly by the following morning, Tuesday, there was no sign of water. At eleven o'clock I photographed again the views of the previous afternoon for comparison. You had to look closely for

June 25, about 3 p.m.   *Next day, 11 a.m.*
Two views of Hornbeam Drive from the Loatley Green junction looking towards Hornbeam Walk. (Pat Elliott)

June 25, about 3 p.m.   *Next day, 11 a.m.*
Two views of Hornbeam Drive from no 30 looking up the lane. (Pat Elliott)

evidence of where the water had been. A line of flotsam on some grass indicated the high water mark.

June 26. The high water mark debris on an open area in Hornbeam Drive. (Pat Elliott)

Mrs Amos, who lives at the head of the lane, told me that the water from Mill Beck, which is culverted, had overflowed in Snuff Mill Lane through a manhole cover and, taking the route of least resistance, flowed down Hall Walk, through the end gardens, and cascaded into her garden and road, being situated lower. The water rose up to the air bricks of her bungalow and into her garage by the rear so that she had to open the garage door for it to escape at the front. Water gushed through the open brickwork of the adjacent boundary wall into the road. This had been the source of our 'river'. Further down Hornbeam Drive, at the

June 26, about 11 a.m. A garden wall at the head of Hornbeam Drive showing the water line under the lower decorative bricks. (Pat Elliott)

June 26. The manhole cover where a minor beck joins the 'Mill Beck' sewer in Snuff Mill Lane. The overflow from this was the chief source of the flooding in Hornbeam Drive. (Pat Elliott)

June 26, midday. Abandoned cars in a still flooded Cottingham Station car park. (Pat Elliott)

junction with Snuff Mill Lane footpath, a house and garage had been flooded, with its land to the rear which stretches to the railway line transformed into a lake. Apart from being adjacent to Mill Beck it appeared to be situated at the lowest point in the area — seemingly this was where our 'river' had ended up.

If Mill Beck had flooded here, what had happened to it in its earlier reaches? John and I decided to investigate, taking a route which we had walked only the previous Friday. As we walked along we became acutely aware of any rise or fall, however slight, in the landscape. We had never noticed that Snuff Mill Lane gradually rises from Snuff Mill House then drops away as it approaches Newgate/ Thwaite Street. There were clear signs of where the water had erupted from the manhole cover. The open beck at the side of 'The Arches' was very high and fast-flowing and there was standing water across Hall Walk.

Keith Hague, the proprietor of Beck Bank News, informed us that the critical time for him had been 10 p.m. on the Monday evening, when the water had reached the step of his business but fortunately no further. Ted Jefferson told us that Mrs Yandall, in a ground floor flat at St Mary's Mount, experienced water seeping in at a similar time and had to evacuate. The car park at the railway station was flooded and had abandoned cars. Most of the businesses down Station Road had standing water outside them.

In Dunswell Road Creyke Beck was full to the brim, with signs of road damage outside 'The Mallards'. Properties on both sides of the road had been affected. On the eastern side were sandbags and channels cut into the verges in the attempt to divert the water away from property. Water was being

Creyke Beck, full to the brim, looking south from Cassandra House, Dunswell Road. (Pat Elliott)

June 26. Water being pumped out on the east side of Dunswell Road, only for it to flow down North Moor Lane (left, line of sandbags beyond the cars). (Pat Elliott)

June 26, midday. Near the junction of Dunswell Road and North Moor Lane, water was still forcing its way out of the manhole cover. (Pat Elliott)

June 26, midday. Mill Beck from the Mill Beck Lane footpath, high but within its banks, though it had obviously been higher (over the footpath). (Pat Elliott)

June 26, midday. Mill Beck where it is culverted beneath Mill Beck Lane. (Pat Elliott)

pumped out only for it to flow down North Moor Lane, as did water still emitting from a manhole cover. An owner on the western side said that the flooding had occurred at ten o'clock the previous night. Surprisingly one property in Wanlass Drive had not been affected.

At Mill Beck Lane, the beck was within its banks but had obviously been higher (over the footpath) and the training ground to the east was flooded. The head of Canongate had water standing in the T turning area, with Mill Beck and Creyke Beck again within their banks but only just below the footbridge. Further along at Caukeel Lane footbridge, boarding had been cut away on the western side to release the pressure of water, and the boundary wall of the first property on the left in Broad Lane Close showed the level to which the water had risen. [See Harold Mankel's story, Central Cottingham, page 100.]

The footbridge at the junction of Mill Beck and Creyke Beck, near the end of Canongate and the 'Danish Bacon' site.

June 26, midday. Mill Beck looking west through the railings of Caukeel Lane bridge (with boarding partially removed). (Pat Elliott)

June 25. Water level between the second and third rungs of the footbridge rails, twenty inches above the footpath. The beck was about 5 feet higher than usual. (John Horsley)

June 26, midday. The waters are back within their banks but are still very high, only just below the footbridge. (Pat Elliott)

Mr Follett's garden (between Kirby Drive, Mill Beck and Caukeel Lane) on the eastern side of the snicket had flooded up to the raspberry canes, with flotsam on the footpath itself denoting that the high water mark had been beyond the lamp-post, past the bend in the school wall.

Back on the main road, at the Newgate Street/Priory Road roundabout, the police were preventing traffic from going down Priory Road, unless you were a resident, with Priory Road completely closed beyond Hornbeam Drive due to the flooding, which had also affected the police station. This route was to remain closed for a few days.

In the afternoon, after an abortive attempt to reach Tesco on Beverley Road, when I was turned away down Hall Road, I walked further east in the village. The grounds of Thwaite Hall, again somewhere I had visited only the previous week, displayed considerable flooding, with water extending to the corner of the wall holding back the garden and terrace, adjacent to the students' residences The top of the jetty in the lake was barely visible. Speaking to two of the gardeners they reported that, despite the inlet at the north-west corner being closed, the water had found its way in, hence the extensive flooding. An old chestnut tree in the woodland had been a casualty.

June 26. Four views of the lake in Thwaite Gardens. (Pat Elliott)

The lake submerging the lawn.

The waters reached the retaining wall (left) of the garden adjacent to student accommodation.

A view of the gardens from the eastern end.

The lake spread over a much greater area than usual.

The northern boundary of 'Boardside' snicket was flooded at either end, that at New Village Road causing heavy spray as drivers were surprised by the water.

June 26. An affected property on the north side of Endyke Lane. The sandbags were delivered by the Council on June 26. (Pat Elliott)

June 26, about 4.30 p.m. A driver surprised by flood water on New Village Road at the east end of Boardside Walk. (Pat Elliott)

Properties on the northern side of Endyke Lane showed that Council sandbagging had been to no avail and pumping out was being done in some properties. Evidence around a manhole cover suggested that water welling up was the cause. The old cottage at no. 25 stood in a sea of water. The Wishing Well Day Nursery and Christ Church also appeared to have been affected.

June 26. No. 25, the last surviving 'Pauper's Cottage' in Endyke Lane from the New Village Settlement (built between 1819 and 1839) still surrounded by water. (Pat Elliott)

The rough ground of the fields beyond was the resting place of much of the water.

June 26. Flooded waste ground on the north side of Endyke Lane. (Pat Elliott)

I made my way back via Dunswell Road and Caukeel Lane photographing more scenes.

June 26, about 5 p.m. Mill Beck from Caukeel Lane footbridge. Note the depth of the water. (Pat Elliott)

June 26. Mill Beck behind Hallgate Junior School. The Broadlane Beck culvert, which discharges into Mill Beck, is just visible (left). (Pat Elliott)

June 26, about 5 p.m. Caukeel Lane looking up towards Hallgate. Note the flotsam strewn across the path and the high water mark on the brick wall. (Pat Elliott)

The playground at Hallgate Junior School had mud and debris, presumably from Mill Beck, which was still running high but within its banks.

June 26, about 5.30 p.m. Looking south at Hallgate Junior School playground covered in mud and debris. Mill Beck runs behind the railings. (Pat Elliott)

With one shot left I ended at the site of the new cemetery down Priory Road, just to record the standing water there.

June 26, late afternoon. Standing water in the field east of Priory Road, the site of Kingston upon Hull's new cemetery. (Pat Elliott)

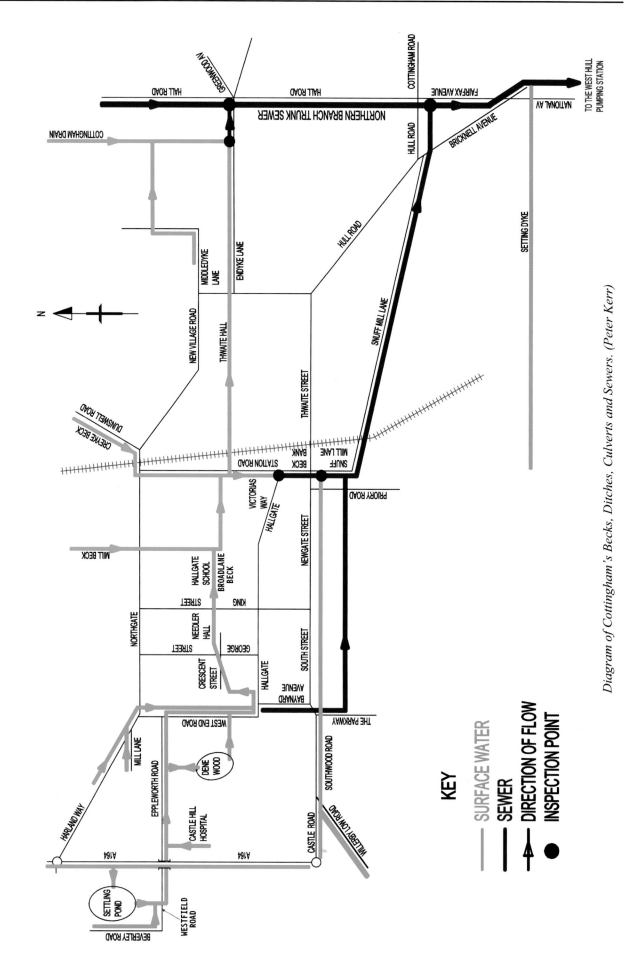

Diagram of Cottingham's Becks, Ditches, Culverts and Sewers. (Peter Kerr)

KEY

— SURFACE WATER

— SEWER

↑ DIRECTION OF FLOW

● INSPECTION POINT

APPENDIX

The Cottingham Drainage System and some Proposals for Preventing Future Flooding

Peter Kerr

We have all recognised that from time to time Cottingham is a very wet place to live. During and after heavy rainfall enormous amounts of water pour down the slopes of the Wolds into Cottingham. The capacity of the principal watercourses (the open becks and some of the ditches) is large and generally adequate. However, the drainage system of culverts and sewers that take the water out of the village has a much smaller capacity, which is the main reason why flooding occurs. The solution is either to slow down the rate at which water comes into the village (by building more flood storage systems such as settling ponds and attenuating reservoirs) and/or to speed up the rate at which water leaves the village, by increasing the culvert and sewer capacity.

The Aquifer

Cottingham is on the eastern slopes of the Yorkshire Wolds, which are formed from chalk. Chalk is both porous and permeable. Chalk forms the principal groundwater reservoirs (aquifers) in the UK.

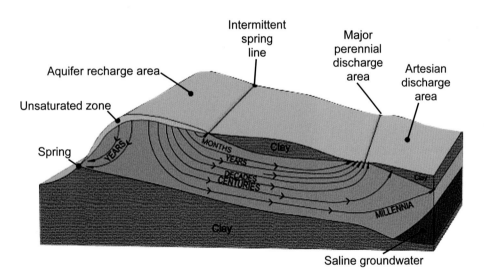

Typical Aquifer

Around fifty percent of the potable water supplied to Hull and the surrounding area, including Cottingham, Willerby, Hessle, etc. is supplied from the aquifer. The water is pumped out of wells cut through the overlying clay into the aquifer at Cottingham, Anlaby (Spring Head) and Dunswell.

The Becks

There are three becks that run through the village. They are supplied with runoff water from the land and water from the aquifer. The flows in the becks can fluctuate between extremes.

Creyke Beck (probably named after the Creyke family, which had an estate in the parish in the 16th and 17th centuries) runs along the west side of Dunswell Road. It is culverted under the

Creyke Beck on Dunswell Road passing into the double culvert under the Northgate railway crossing. (Peter Kerr)

railway line and across Northgate at the level crossing. The culvert flows into a ditch behind Crossing Cottage on the corner of Station Road. Creyke Beck joins the water from Mill Beck and Broadlane Beck at the footbridge on the snicket that runs from Station Road to Caukeel Lane and Hallgate.

Mill Beck (also known as Cottingham Beck) was once used to power two water mills, North Mill and South Mill. South Mill later became known as Snuff Mill. Mill Beck is culverted behind Mill Beck Lane. The culvert runs under the footpath on the east side of the lane. The culvert passes under Northgate and Canongate and emerges in a ditch at the eastern end of the Hallgate School playing field, where it is joined by Broadlane Beck and later by Creyke Beck.

Broadlane Beck is perhaps less well known, because it is almost entirely culverted. It seems to have had its origin somewhere in the springs on Eppleworth Road and may have been a source of water to the moat at Baynard Castle. It is presently fed by water from the ditch in Harland Way, the culverted ditches on both sides of Eppleworth Road and Dene pond, all of which is

The culvert (1.2m dia.) and screen behind Mill Beck Lane. (Peter Kerr)

The Broadlane Beck culvert (1.2m dia.) at King's Court, King Street, looking east. (Peter Kerr)

culverted under West End Road into Hallgate, where it flows into a ditch behind and parallel with the footpath. From the eastern end of the ditch the water is culverted along the route of the old Broadlane Beck, down Crescent Street, across George Street and into George Place where it once again flows into a ditch. From there a culvert carries the water through the grounds of Needler Hall, after which it enters a ditch at Kings Court. A culvert at the eastern end of Kings Court takes the water under King Street and across the

Two culverts (750mm dia.) decanting water from Broadlane Beck into Mill Beck behind Broad Lane Close, on the east side of Hallgate School playing field. (Peter Kerr)

Footbridge over Creyke Beck at its junction with Mill Beck. (Peter Kerr)

Hallgate School playing field where it joins Mill Beck, behind Broad Lane Close. The two watercourses, now combined, continue eastward to join Creyke Beck at the footbridge near Canongate on the snicket that runs from Hallgate to Station Road. The water from the three becks, after passing through a 'rough' screen at Victoria's Way, decants into the public sewer at the junction of Hallgate, Station Road and Beck Bank. Some of the water from the combined becks, near Victoria's Way, is culverted into the

university grounds of Thwaite Hall, where it feeds into the western end of the lake. At the eastern end of the lake a valve controls the level of water in the lake by admitting the surplus water into a culvert that crosses New Village Road and runs under the footpath on the north side of Endyke Lane to the electricity substation, where it merges with the culverted Cottingham Drain.

The rough screen at Victoria's Way, where Mill Beck decants via a 900mm diameter culvert into the 1050mm public sewer on Hallgate. (Peter Kerr)

Outlet control valve from Thwaite Lake. (Peter Kerr)

The Eppleworth Valley

The Eppleworth Valley, from Rowley to eastern side of Cottingham, was cut by melt water after the last ice age. Over a distance of 6.5 kilometres, the valley falls around seventy metres. During the heavy rain on 25th June 2007, the water followed the route the melt water would have taken. It flowed down the valley and along Eppleworth Road, cut across West End Road, flowed through the grounds at Hillcrest House, along Crescent Street (west), across George Street, King Street and the Hallgate School playing field to join Mill Beck at the eastern end of the playing field.

The valley is still evident in the middle of the village, indicated by the dip in the road on George Street and to a lesser extent in King Street. After King Street the melt water had spent most of its force, and the gravel, sand and other sediments began to form a plain.

The settling pond near the A164, Eppleworth Road underpass, after some overnight rain. (Peter Kerr)

The A164 Beverley Road

The A164 road, between Castle Road and Harland Way, is drained into a settling pond adjacent to the road, near to the Eppleworth Road underpass. This section of the A164 has an area of around 1.8 hectares (one hectare is 10,000 square metres). A simple calculation shows that 50mm of rain produces 900 cubic metres (around 200,000 gallons) of water. The settling pond holds around 2,000 cubic metres of water.

The water from the settling pond discharges via a french drain (a trench filled with stone with possibly a perforated or porous pipe beneath) to an inspection chamber under the bypass. The chamber on the south side of Eppleworth Road has 1000mm diameter concrete culvert sections in and out, which convey the water from Westfield Road (Eppleworth, the road to the west of the Eppleworth Road underpass) into the Eppleworth Road surface water system.

The Eppleworth Road Surface Water System

The culvert opens out into a ditch after it emerges from under the underpass. A 750mm diameter culvert links the ditch on the north side of the road to the ditch on the south side of the road.

The Castle Hill Hospital attenuation ditch, looking west to the Oncology Unit building. (16.07.08) (Tony Grundy)

An attenuation ditch was constructed near to the Castle Hill northern boundary when the oncology unit was built. The ditch collects the surface water from the oncology unit impermeable surfaces and slowly discharges the water into the roadside ditch on the south side of Eppleworth Road, regulated to 10 litres per second. At the eastern boundary of the Castle Hill Hospital the water from the Eppleworth Road ditches enters a 750mm diameter concrete culvert. A ditch running along the hospital's eastern boundary is connected into the culvert. This surface water source is unregulated.

A brick built culvert, around 1000mm in diameter, cross connects the ditch on the north side of Eppleworth Road to the culvert on the south side of the road, outside no. 159.

Eastern outlet from the attenuation ditch discharging into the ditch on Eppleworth Road, looking south. (Peter Kerr)

The 750mm diameter concrete culvert at an inspection chamber adjacent to Dene wood is cross connected via a 200mm diameter balancing pipe to the pond in Dene wood.

The ditch on the north side of Eppleworth Road enters a 450mm diameter culvert outside no. 22. The last inspection chamber on the north side of Eppleworth Road is round the corner from no. 35 West End Road. The culvert leaving the pipe is only 300mm in diameter. This culvert connects to a brick built culvert that crosses Eppleworth Road into the last inspection chamber on the south side of Eppleworth Road.

The culvert from the south side of Eppleworth Road runs under West End Road and turns south in the inspection chamber on West End Road directly opposite the inspection chamber on the south side of Eppleworth Road. The culvert follows West End Road and decants into a ditch on Hallgate outside no. 286.

Harland Way Surface Water System

The old Ordnance Survey maps show a ditch on the north side of Harland Way. The only part of the ditch that remains runs in front of the houses on The Woodlands. Water from Mill Lane (off Harland Way) probably joins the water from Harland Way somewhere around this point.

The ditch in Hallgate after overnight rain, looking west to the culvert from West End Road. (Peter Kerr)

The water is culverted under the access road to The Lawns and flows into a short length of ditch. The water flows south from the ditch in a 450mm diameter culvert. It runs under Northgate and along the eastern side of West End Road. It runs parallel with the culvert from Eppleworth Road. The two culverts merge in an inspection chamber on the south east corner of West End Road. The surface water from Harland Way and Mill Lane decants into the ditch on Hallgate, along with the water from the Eppleworth Road surface water system.

The ditch and culvert (225mm dia.) on Mill Lane. (Peter Kerr)

Ditch and culvert (450mm dia.) at the entrance to the Lawns, turning south under Northgate and along the eastern side of West End Road. (Peter Kerr)

The Castle Road Surface Water System

The Castle Road system carries water from the surrounding fields, the ditch on Willerby Low Road, some of the hard surfaces in the Castle Hill Hospital and some of the surface water from the road gullies on Castle Road.

The culvert runs along the south side of Southwood Road. At the junction of Southwood Road and The Parkway the culvert crosses under The Parkway and decants into an open ditch at the back of no. 1 Arncliffe Way. The ditch runs behind the houses on Arncliffe Way to an inspection chamber on Brookland Park (house no. 1). The water crosses Brookland Park in four, 450mm diameter culverts into another inspection chamber (house no. 8). The outgoing culvert is 1000mm in diameter.

The cross section and shape of the culvert changes as it makes its way across the south side of the village. The culvert passes through Cottage Green (off The Garth). There is an inspection chamber in the back garden of no. 4. The culvert runs under the Bacon Garth school playing field to an inspection chamber in the back garden of no. 35 Cedar Avenue, where it turns 90 degrees to the north.

Culvert from Southwood Road entering the ditch behind no. 1 Arncliffe Way, looking west (17.03.08). (Peter Kerr)

Culvert into the ditch behind 31 Longman's Lane, looking north (28.03.08). (Peter Kerr)

The next inspection chamber is on Bacon Garth Lane, where the culvert turns 90 degrees to the east. There is an inspection chamber in The Spinney (house no. 3). The next inspection chamber is in the road on Oakdene.

At this point the culvert is rectangular is section. It runs between houses (nos. 21 and 23) to Longmans Lane (no. 9), where over a distance of around five metres it turns through two right angles and continues eastward. There are another three inspection chambers on Longmans Lane (the last one in the drive of house no. 31). The culvert discharges into a ditch which runs behind the houses on Priory Crescent.

The water from the ditch decants into a culvert on Priory Road (between no. 14 Priory Road and the

Ditch to the north of 14 Priory Road, looking west (28.03.08). (Peter Kerr)

Culvert into the ditch south of The Arches, Priory Road, looking east (28.03.08). (Peter Kerr)

electricity sub-station). After crossing the road the culvert discharges into a ditch that runs along the southern boundary of The Arches (a residential care home).

The ditch runs through to Yorkshire Water's fresh water inlet on Snuff Mill Lane. The water is culverted under Snuff Mill Lane to an inspection chamber on the east side of the lane.

The inspection chamber connects into the public sewer on Snuff Mill Lane via two pipes. The watercourse that discharges

Yorkshire Water's fresh water inlet on the west side of Snuff Mill Lane (20.03.08). (Peter Kerr)

into the inspection chamber has a capacity equal to at least a 750mm diameter culvert from the point at which it crosses the Parkway, whereas the two pipes are only 400mm and 250mm respectively. After heavy rainfall it is inevitable that the water will sometimes back up.

Cottingham Branch Sewer

The surface water from the north and west of the village is conveyed by Mill Beck, Creyke Beck and Broadlane Beck to 'Victoria's Beck' (i.e. Mill Beck at Victoria's Way), where it discharges into the public sewer at the junction of Hallgate, Station Road and Beck Bank. The sewer follows the route of the old beck along Beck Bank, crosses Newgate Street to run under the grassed area on the east side of Snuff Mill Lane (north).

The water from the Castle Road surface water system discharges into the public sewer at the inspection chamber on Snuff Mill Lane, near Hall Walk. The sewer runs to the west of Snuff Mill House, runs under Hornbeam Drive to join with another incoming sewer on Snuff Mill Lane (south). A third sewer connects into the public sewer (at no. 16 Hornbeam Drive). The single sewer continues along the east

side of Snuff Mill Lane. After crossing under the railway line, the sewer crosses to the west side of Snuff Mill Lane. The sewer crosses Bricknell Avenue, runs along the south side of Hull Road and connects into the Northern Branch trunk sewer at Fairfax Avenue.

At the eastern end of the village, the surface water from the ditches on Northmoor Lane and Middledyke Lane decants into the Cottingham Drain. The Cottingham Drain connects into the public sewer system on Endyke Lane, near the electricity sub station. The public sewer decants into the Northern Branch trunk sewer at the junction of Endyke Lane, Greenwood Avenue and Hall Road.

Ditch with rubbish in Middledyke Lane at the culvert leading to Cottingham Drain. (Peter Kerr)

Northern Branch Trunk Sewer

The Northern Branch trunk sewer, constructed under the 'West Hull and Haltemprice Joint Main Drainage' scheme in the 1950s, conveys all the sewage and surface water to the West Hull Pumping Station, which was built at the same time and was part of the scheme.

Western Branch Trunk Sewer

The Western Branch trunk sewer, constructed under the same scheme as the Northern Branch trunk sewer, conveys the sewage and surface water from Hessle, Anlaby, Willerby, etc. to the West Hull Pumping Station.

West Hull Sewers

Two sewers, which convey the sewage and surface water from the area around west Hull, cascade into the Northern and Western branch trunk sewers adjacent to the West Hull Pumping Station. The trunk sewers, where they discharge into the mixing chamber at the West Hull Pumping Station, are 3.27m (Northern Branch) and 2.4m in diameter (Western Branch).

West Hull Pumping Station

The West Hull Pumping Station, inaugurated in 1957, for almost fifty years pumped the sewage and surface water into the River Humber. The station has eight storm pumps and four dry weather flow pumps. Two of the storm pumps are driven by diesel engines. The other pumps were driven by electric motors. The station had a maximum pumping capacity of 32 cubic metres per second. The water from the West Hull Pumping Station now flows into the Humbercare tunnel, restricted to 14 cubic metres per second via a vortex flow restrictor, which is less than half the earlier pumping capacity.

East Hull Pumping Station

The East Hull Pumping Station is similar to the West Hull Pumping Station. Large sewers convey sewage and surface water to the station, from where it used to be discharged into the River Humber. It had a total pumping capacity of 26 cubic metres per second. The water from the East Hull Pumping Station now flows into the Humbercare tunnel, restricted to 8 cubic metres per second via a vortex flow restrictor, which is less than a third of the earlier pumping capacity.

The Humbercare Tunnel

Due to EU legislation, water companies had to stop the practice of pumping untreated sewage into rivers. The water from the West Hull and East Hull pumping stations is now transferred under gravity (not pumped) via the Humbercare tunnel to the Waste Water Treatment Works at Saltend. The tunnel, construction of which was finished in 2001, is 3.6m in diameter, 10.7km long and has a fall over its whole length of 7m. The tunnel is used for storage. When full it holds almost 110,000 cubic metres of water.

Saltend Waste Water Treatment Works

The waste water treatment works can fully treat 6 cubic metres of sewage per second and partially treat 12 cubic metres of sewage per second. The remaining sewage, after being screened, is pumped directly into the River Humber. The waste water treatment works has a maximum pumping capacity of 22 cubic metres per second.

Flood Risk and the Sewerage System

The disposal of sewage and surface water from Cottingham, Hessle, Anlaby, Willerby, etc. is inextricably linked to the operation of the East and West Hull pumping stations, the correct operation of the Humbercare tunnel, the functionality and pumping capacity of the Saltend Waste Water Treatment Works.

The final report of Hull City's Independent Review Body (November 21, 2007, pp. 61—2) found that:-

For West and East Hull, where there was extensive flooding in 2007, Yorkshire Water reports from 2004, 2006 and 2007 indicated that the new £200 million 'Humbercare' system had actually reduced the drainage and pumping capacity of Hull. Detailed Modelling in 2004 and 2006 showed that the new Humbercare design had underestimated the volume of water from some storms by 100%. In 2004 the system was only providing protection from a 1 in 1 to 1 in 2 year flood event instead of protection from a 1 in 30 year event. Options for permanent solutions to this problem were presented to Yorkshire Water in 2004 and 2006.

In 2007, 2½ years after the initial report detailing these issues, Yorkshire Water implemented a temporary solution based on bolting on the de-commissioned 40 year old pumping stations at West and East Hull. During the 2007 floods there were serious operational issues with this arrangement (notably the poor reliability of old pumps and oscillations developing in the main Humbercare transfer tunnel) and we have significant concerns as to whether the system performed correctly. We understand that plans for a permanent solution are now being pursued after the June floods. We feel that had the permanent solutions suggested in 2004 and 2006 been implemented by the time of the June floods, the impact of the floods would not have been as severe.

On 20th November 2007, Yorkshire Water announced that it had re-prioritised other investment to provide £16m to improve its assets in Hull. The money was to be spent on improvements to the Bransholme pumping station and at the East and West Hull pumping stations on upgrading and replacement of pumps and civil engineering projects to enhance flows into the stations.

Eppleworth Road Underpass: Proposed Impounding Reservoir

If you are not able to increase the rate at which water leaves the village, you must slow down the rate at which it enters the village if flooding is to be avoided. Water flowing down the Eppleworth valley on 25th June 2007 contributed to the flooding of many homes in the village. The culverts, ditches and sewers were inundated with water. Some of the worst affected properties were those adjacent to the Eppleworth valley and those on the route the melt water would have taken after the last ice age. These include properties on West End Road, George Street, King Street, etc.

There is a partial man-made barrier across the Eppleworth valley, where the A164 Beverley Road crosses Eppleworth Road. Had it been possible to stop the water here, a good deal of the flooding in the village that occurred on 25th June 2007 could have been avoided.

The underpass on Eppleworth Road resembles a defensible 'gate', similar to those found in once walled towns like York, Lincoln, etc. These towns were surrounded by stout walls. The gates were the points of access to the towns. Similarly, adjacent to the underpass, the sides of the Eppleworth valley rise steeply to the north and south to form stout 'walls'. The underpass is the point of access.

For operational reasons, a watertight gate built across the Eppleworth Road underpass would not be practical. However, it would be possible to intercept and impound the water at the underpass. A grid the full width of the road could be constructed under the underpass. Water flowing down the valley would fall through the grid into a concrete tank. The water could be led away from the tank to an impounding reservoir. Water from the ditches and culverts on Westfield Road (Eppleworth) could also be diverted into the impounding reservoir. The water from the impounding reservoir could be decanted, at a controlled rate and at a suitable elevation to the existing culvert on the south side of Eppleworth Road.

Eppleworth Road to the west of the underpass is around 31m AOD (Above Ordnance Datum, above the mean sea level at Newlyn, Cornwall). A culvert inspection chamber outside no. 159 Eppleworth Road is 19m AOD. Due to the gradient of Eppleworth Road it would be possible to discharge the water at a point more than ten metres below the collecting point. It would therefore, depending on the geology, be possible to construct a deep impounding reservoir, thus reducing the surface area needed to contain a specified volume of water.

The proposed grid would not impede the flow of traffic. The water would be confined by the walls of the underpass, thus preventing water bypass. The proposed structure would require minimum maintenance. It would function without the need for human intervention and would safeguard the village from flooding from the Eppleworth valley.

Proposals for Rerouting the Surface Water

On the east side of Cottingham a short term fix could be effected by diverting some of the water from Creyke Beck to the Cottingham Drain.

On the west side, due to the heavy rainfall on June 25th, the water that accumulated on Eppleworth Road flooded many houses. The water pressure in the surcharged culvert under Crescent Street (west) forced the covers off the inspection points. The water escaping from the inspection points contributed to the flooding of Crescent Street and George Street.

To prevent the flooding on the west side of the village, some or all of the surface water culverted from Eppleworth Road and Mill Lane could be diverted into an adjacent sewer at the junction of West End Road, Hallgate and Baynard Avenue. The sewer runs south under Baynard Avenue, Southwood Road and The Parkway. It turns east along Yedingham Walk, runs under Fimber Avenue, crosses the fields and Priory Road. It merges with the Cottingham Branch sewer at Hornbeam Drive and Snuff Mill Lane. Routing the surface water via this more direct route to the Northern Branch trunk sewer (avoiding the tortuous route through the middle of the village) would reduce the risk of flooding.

However, the Cottingham Branch sewer is inadequate. Unless someone takes the step to increase the capacity of the sewer, flooding will remain a perennial problem in Cottingham.

Global Warming

Some people suppose that the flooding in June 2007 was due to global warming. The Centre for Ecology & Hydrology has determined that it was not. In a recently published 32 page report they say:-

> *A synthesis of the rainfall and river flow evidence indicates that the summer was a very singular episode. The associated fluvial flooding does not constitute an element in any established hydrological trend or appear to form part of a pattern consistent with currently favoured climate change scenarios.*
>
> Marsh, T. J. and Hannaford, J., *The summer 2007 floods in England and Wales — a hydrological appraisal,* Centre for Ecology & Hydrology (2007), p. 4.

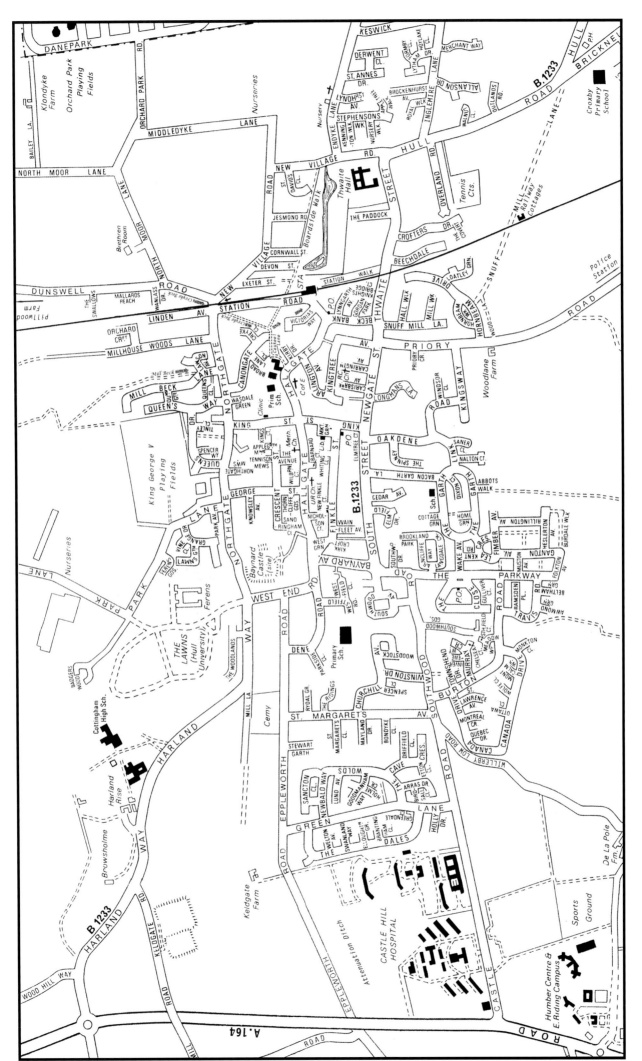

Map of the Cottingham area. (Reproduced with permission of C J Utting)

Cottingham Local History Society

Cottingham Local History Society has been flourishing for over 50 years. It was the brainchild of John Whitehouse, who in 1952 advertised for people interested in forming a society. From the initial nine who responded our membership has grown, so much so that in the early 1990s our meetings were moved from the small room in the Civic Hall, Market Green, to Hallgate Junior School, coincidentally the venue of early Society meetings.

From October 2008 we shall meet on the first Wednesday of the month in the Red Hall, Hallgate Primary School, Cottingham, at 7.45 p.m. from October to April inclusive. Our programme of talks, often slide presentations, endeavours to cover aspects associated with the East Riding, with specific reference to Cottingham wherever possible. In addition visits are arranged during the summer period and our regular publication, *The Cottingham Local History Society Journal*, is provided as part of the subscription fee of Single £6.00 and Double £11.00 (for 2008–9). There is a meeting fee of £1 for members and £2 for visitors.

In 2002 the Society set up its Historic Cottingham Project with the help of funding from the Local Heritage Initiative. One of its aims was to create digitally recorded archives of photographs and of oral memories of life in Cottingham. These are still ongoing and new contributions are always welcome. Other aims were to research and compile a book, *Cottingham in the 20th Century*, published in 2005 and now out of print, and a heritage trail leaflet, *Historic Cottingham Walk*, published in 2006 and still available from the Society and from outlets in the village (Barker's in Hallgate, Cottingham Library, pubs, etc.). The work of the Project continues with the present book. The Society also publishes materials such as postcards, greetings cards and booklets, which are usually on sale at the meetings.

The Society welcomes new members. If you are interested in joining, please contact the Treasurer, Mr Anthony Barron, 76 Millhouse Woods Lane, Cottingham, HU16 4HB, or the Chairman, Mr Peter McClure, 47 West End Road, Cottingham, HU16 5PW, tel. 01482 845734. For information on meetings look out for our advertisements in Cottingham Library, on Parish Council notice boards and in the *Hull Daily Mail*.

The Society's badge is taken from the coat of arms that was granted in 1952 to the Haltemprice Urban District Council (1935–1974). The Council and its district were named after an Augustinian priory founded in 1322 by Thomas Wake, then lord of Cottingham. Building began on land south of Northgate in Cottingham, but because of legal disputes about the ownership of the land the priory was rebuilt in 1324 at Newton, a hamlet that once lay between Cottingham and Willerby. The name 'Haltemprice' is from Old French *haulte emprise*, meaning 'high enterprise' or 'noble endeavour'.